THE BOOK
OF PRACTICAL
Witchcraft

THE BOOK OF PRACTICAL
Witchcraft

A compendium of spells, rituals and occult knowledge

Pamela Ball

SIRIUS

All images courtesy of Shutterstock

SIRIUS

This edition published in 2023 by Sirius Publishing, a division of
Arcturus Publishing Limited,
26/27 Bickels Yard, 151–153 Bermondsey Street,
London SE1 3HA

ISBN: 978-1-3988-2847-6
AD010851US

Printed in China

CONTENTS

HARM NONE

Lest we be accused of undue influence, as have others
before us, we hereby take responsibility for the words
written within the pages of this book. We do not, however,
take any responsibility for your performance of the spells and
rituals herein nor for the results of the use of the Powers. Such
performance and result is a transaction between you and those
Powers, for which you yourself must take responsibility.
We trust that this book will help you in your search for
understanding and offer a blessing to help you on your way.

May the Divine be with you.
May you always be guided,
guarded and protected.

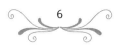

INTRODUCTION

The desire to change and improve our situation has been around for many thousands of years, if not since humans first walked the earth. Magic and spell-working have always been a part of that, and still are. Anyone who practices any form of magic, including spell-working, needs to be grounded. This means having both feet firmly planted in reality and having a basic knowledge of what magic is and is not, what spells can and can't do, and what—with practice—you can do with the tools, information and knowledge you have. This book aims to give you that information in as succinct a manner as possible.

It is sometimes best not to attempt any definition of ancient magic and magical belief. However, in any discussion of magic and its practitioners, we must take account of a period in which the magical traditions of different cultures coalesced and merged into a type of international and even multicultural magical practice with its own rituals, symbols, and words of power. This occurred in the Mediterranean basin and the Near East from the 1st to the 7th centuries, and is the basis of most of the early, more intellectually based, systems of magic.

The pursuit of magic is, in part, the result of the human desire for control. In this period there was a need to control the natural environment, the social world, and the outcome of forces we did not fully understand. This underlying desire for control comes to the surface most often in times of change, as we have seen repeatedly over the last fifteen centuries. During this time the techniques may have been modified, but the goals have remained the same. The basic laws of magic, of control, apply today, just as they always have.

A BRIEF HISTORY OF WITCHCRAFT

For millennia, humans have looked to the stars for guidance, and the spirit world for inspiration. Our ancestors worshipped gods who, they believed, looked after the spirits of those who had died and gone to live in the spirit world. In many cultures, a shaman performed rituals and made magic, and it is fair to say that some magical elements survive in the religions of today.

Over centuries, religions developed in which magic played a central part, and both magic and religion depend on ritual. The religions of Ancient Egypt, Greece and Rome, the Celtic world and the Scandinavian countries all had magic in some form at their core.

The Celts, the Druids and Paganism

Many people believe that modern witchcraft has Celtic roots. The deeply spiritual and pantheistic Celts (700BCE–100CE) honored the "Divine Creator of all Nature" and worshipped the "One Creative Life Source."

Celtic rites and rituals were supervised by the Druids. These spiritual leaders were regarded not just as priests; they were judges, teachers, astrologers, healers, bards and ambassadors who passed from one warring tribe to another to settle disputes.

Nature and the seasons governed the Celts' religious year, and their beliefs grew into what became known as Paganism. Their rituals then blended with the ways of others, and such practices as concocting lotions and potions, performing works of magic and casting spells developed.

The Old Ways vs. Christianity

As the Roman empire expanded and brought its own rituals and beliefs, the number of Druids dwindled. And with the birth of Christianity, old gods were banished and the new religion imposed.

However, the old rituals, beliefs and traditions continued to be handed down from generation to generation; Pagans, practicing these traditions in defiance of the Church, risked persecution and death.

The Inquisition and Witch Hunts

In 1484, Pope Innocent VIII condemned the practice of witchcraft, and called upon every Roman Catholic (which meant almost everyone, as the Church was so powerful) to help his inquisitors search out witches.

Thousands were accused of witchcraft all over Europe and, later, in European colonies in the New World. Torture was often used to force a confession out of an

innocent person and, in almost every case, the accused confessed and was sentenced to death.

Fortunately, with the emergence of scientific, rational thought in 18th-century Europe, witchcraft was perceived as little more than superstition. Eventually witch hunts came to an end and witchcraft ceased to be a crime.

Witchcraft Today and Wicca

In 1954, Gerald Gardner published *Witchcraft Today,* in which he advocated the use of old rituals and introduced many of his own. His work has links to ancient Paganism: the use of high magic, the use of plants and herbs in spells, and the involvement of folk rites and customs to manipulate the powers of nature.

Gardner is credited by many as the founder of what is now an officially recognized religion: Wicca. This modern Pagan religion, which has followers all over the world, honors The God and The Goddess as the two main deities.

Wiccans practice various forms of magic and perform rituals to attune themselves with the natural rhythms of life forces, particularly those marked by the phases of the moon and the four seasons.

Other cultures

Witchcraft exists among many cultures and indigenous peoples around the world. In North America, for instance, the Navajo believe that witchcraft is an exclusively male practice; its initiates meet at night, and make magic while wearing nothing except a mask and jewelery. They sit among baskets of corpses and are said to "converse" with dead women.

In other parts of the world, witchcraft is blamed for disease and disaster. The sick might turn to conventional medicine to cure their physical symptoms while also looking to a witch doctor to explain and treat the hidden causes of the illness. They may wear amulets to protect them from disease, practice the divination advised by the witch doctor, and take the "medicine" that is prescribed.

PART I
THE TOOLS

WHAT WILL I NEED?

When performing your spells and magical workings, you will find that you need to understand why you use tools in certain ways. Before learning how to set up your altar (see page 61), here is a list of the most commonly used tools.

Altar Objects

This is a general term for the objects you place on your altar—candleholders, vases and so forth—which do not necessarily have a magical use of their own; they are present to create ambience. Dedicate them to the purpose at hand by presenting them to your chosen deity. You may find it helpful to consult the Deities section (see page 44).

Athame

An athame is a ceremonial knife used in the performing of spells. Its role is ceremonial, for example indicating the quarters or directions. It should be made of the purest metal available. Its handle is usually black and often carved with magical designs and symbols. Many magical practitioners believe the most powerful athame is one that has been inherited.

Besom

A besom is a different name for a broom, and is associated with the so-called "witch's broom" of old. It is a personal tool, and is often made for the practitioner with twigs from the tree of their choice. It is usually used in a sacred space or circle, and is used both symbolically and spiritually.

Boline

The boline is a knife that is traditionally used in cutting plants, herbs, wands and other objects for spells and magical workings. It is akin to the gardener's pruning knife as a useful, practical tool. It often has a white handle and a curved blade. It is consecrated, because this is a way of honoring its purpose.

Burin

A burin is a sharp-pointed instrument used for inscribing candles and other magical objects with symbols, words and pictures in order to make spells more effective. In many ways, it is more useful than either the boline or the athame, and is used more for piercing a surface rather than cutting it.

Candles

Candles are such an integral part of a spell-maker's work that they have become a whole branch of magic all their own. They represent the Element of Fire, but also light. Various colors bring different qualities to magical workings, and they are an important part of any ritual (see pages 22-26).

Cauldron

Because cauldrons were easily disguised as cooking utensils in olden days, people tend to think of them as a large cast-iron pot. Lately, there has been a return to original materials, and today they can be made of almost anything. They are often of a size that can be placed on the altar or in the sacred space. They are used mainly as containers for herbs, candles and other magical objects.

Chalice

Used as a ceremonial drinking vessel, the chalice is sometimes made from precious metal, although it can also be made of glass. An elegant object, the chalice will usually be decorated with jewels and gems, or designs that may have magical significance.

Charcoal

Charcoal is a component of incense and oil burning. Nowadays, the best charcoal is usually found in compressed small discs of about 1 inch (3cm). These give a burning time of approximately 45 minutes.

Compass

While this may seem like an unusual tool, many spells, rituals and techniques require you to honor or face certain directions or compass points in their performance. It is also necessary to know the correct alignment in Feng Shui. The easiest way to figure out the direction is by using a compass. It does not need to be decorative, ornate or expensive.

Incense and Oil Burner

The choice of this tool is a personal matter. An incense burner should give plenty of room to allow the aromas and smoke to disperse. Traditional material, such as brass or clay, may be used. The best shape is slightly flat rather than too concave. Oil burners should be large enough to allow a long enough time to complete your spell. Burners that allow you to float the oil on water, which then evaporates, are probably the safest.

Paper

During spells, you will need to write down your wishes or aims, so it is good to have some paper. Parchment is best, but heavy good-quality paper is perfectly fine. You consecrate it by holding it for a short period in the smoke from your favorite incense.

Pen and Ink

Traditionally, quill pens were used for writing spells and incantations, but if you can't find a quill, use the best pen you can afford. Keep it especially for magical work, and consecrate it by passing it carefully over the top of a candle or through incense. Also buy a good-quality ink and, if not already formulated for magical purposes, consecrate it in the same way. Neither pen nor ink should be used for other purposes.

Pentacle

The pentacle is a shallow dish that is usually inscribed with a pentagram—a five-pointed star. It is used as a "power point" for consecrating other objects such amulets, tools, and water or wine in a chalice.

Pestle and Mortar

The pestle and mortar are so symbolic of the union of God and Goddess that they deserve a special mention. Mainly used to prepare herbal mixtures and incenses, they can also become part of your altar furniture when properly consecrated.

Scrying Tools

Scrying is the practice of using certain channeling tools, which should be consecrated before use—crystals, mirrors, colored water, runes and so forth—to try to gain insight into external events. Any object can be used for scrying, although they are usually reflective, and they employ the arts of concentration and contemplation.

Staff

The staff is used frequently by practitioners, particularly if they are of the Druidic persuasion. Longer than a wand, a staff has the same attributes and uses, and is deliberately fashioned for the practitioner from wood taken from sacred trees, such as oak, hawthorn and hazelnut.

Wand

The wand should be no longer than the forearm and is often made from sacred wood. Since the wand is a personal object, it should be chosen carefully, and equally carefully attuned to your energies. It cannot be used magically until it has been properly consecrated.

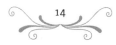

COMPONENTS OF MAGICAL WORKING

Just as a recipe contains ingredients, there are certain components needed in magical workings in order to enhance their power and energy. To the uninitiated, some of these may seem strange, but if we remember that much magic initially had to be performed with what was immediately and easily available to the practitioner, the use of such items makes a great deal of sense. Candles, herbs and so on thus become an important part of modern-day spell-working.

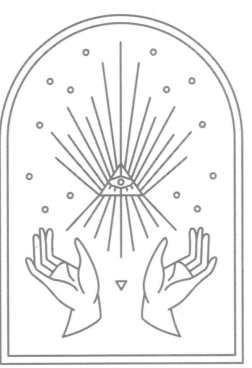

THE ELEMENTS

In most systems of magical working you will find the four (or sometimes five) Elements, often in conjunction with their directions or, as they are known in magic, quarters of the Universe or cardinal points. They are extremely powerful sources of energy and can give a tremendous boost to your spell-making.

The four Elements are energies, and manifestations of energy, that make up the Universe. They also influence our personalities, and therefore what we do. Magical working calls to each Elemental kingdom and its ruler to protect each cardinal point and its properties. Each Element has an intrinsic power and is known for having certain qualities, natures, moods and magical purposes.

The four Elements are Earth, Air, Fire and Water, and you may find that you work best using one of them in particular. People drawn to candle magic, for instance, are using mainly the Element of Fire, while those who work with incense are using Air with a smattering of Earth in the herbs and resins. Oils used in baths for spell-work are using the Element of Water and Earth.

The fifth Element is that of Spirit, the "binding principle" behind everything. Sometimes known as Ether, it is, on the whole, intangible. But it makes everything happen. You are both its representative and its channel, so in magical working you have a responsibility to act wisely and well.

EARTH

Traditionally, the direction of this Element is North and the color associated with it is green. It is usually represented on the altar by salt, sand or stones.

When invoking Earth and the Powers of the North, you are looking for healing and trying to find answers. These Powers deal with knowledge, blessing, creating and shielding. When working in a magical circle, this is the first corner or quarter on which you call for protection.

The principal nature spirits of the Earth are called gnomes. They live underground and guard the Earth's treasures. Other nature spirits ruled by the god Pan are brownies, dryads, earth spirits, elves and satyrs.

AIR

The direction of this Element is East and the color usually associated with it is yellow. Incense is often used to represent Air, since the movement of the air can be seen in the incense smoke.

When you are looking for inspiration, need new ideas, or want to break free from the past or undesired situations, use this Element. The quality associated with it is the intellect. When working in a magical circle, Air is the second quarter on which you call for protection.

The sylphs are the Air spirits; their element has the most subtle energy of the four. They are said to live on the tops

of mountains, and are volatile. They are usually perceived with wings, and look like cherubs or fairies. One of their main spiritual tasks is said to be to help humans receive inspiration.

FIRE

Fire is the Element of the South, and is usually represented by a candle or a cauldron with a fire inside. Its color is red, and its associations are to do with power, determination and passionate energy.

Call upon this Element for protection from evil forces, cleansing and creativity. The quality associated with Fire is "doing," and it is a male principle. It is the third quarter or cardinal point on which you call for protection when working in a magical circle.

Without salamanders, the spirit of fire, it is said that physical fire cannot exist. They have been seen as sparks or small balls of light. They are considered the strongest

and most powerful of all the elementals. As nature spirits, they are greatly affected by the way humankind thinks.

WATER

Water is the Element of the West, and is represented by a bowl of water or a goblet of wine or fruit juice. Its color is blue and, because it represents the giving of life, is associated with sea, rain, snow and rivers.

When you need cleansing, revitalizing, the removal of curses or hexes, or change of any kind, call upon Water. It has to do with emotions, from the most basic passions to the most elevated forms of belief. It is predominantly feminine and is the fourth and final quarter you invoke in any magical circle.

The undines are the elemental beings connected with Water. The nymph is frequently found in a fountain, and the mermaid belongs to the ocean. Some undines inhabit waterfalls, while others live

in rivers and lakes. Small undines are seen as winged beings that people mistakenly call fairies.

SPIRIT

When you feel you are adept at using the other Elements, you may begin to use Spirit—the fifth Element. It has no special space; it is everywhere. It shouldn't be used negatively because, particularly when you are weak and tired, it can rebound on you.

You might find that you instinctively connect with the Life Force as Spirit, in which case you are probably bringing all the Elements together within yourself. There is no particular color associated with Spirit—perception is all-important. If you choose to represent Spirit on the altar, you may do so however you wish. You are free to use your intuition, but you must have a strong awareness of your reason for choosing that symbol, and your connection with it.

DIFFERENT TYPES OF SPELL-WORKING

ELEMENTAL

In this type of magic, the Elements of Fire, Earth, Air and Water are given their own directional focus to create added power and give extra energy to your spells. You will no doubt find that you prefer one direction, but you should be able to use all of them.

COLOR

Perhaps the simplest form of magic is that which involves color. This method of working is also used in combination with other forms of magic.

Color can enhance or change moods and emotions, and can therefore be used to represent our chosen goal. At its simplest, it can be used alone, for example, when dressing an altar.

HERBAL

Herbal magic is often used alongside other forms of magic. Used as talismans and amulets—for example, in a pouch or bag—herbs become protective; the oils from herbs can also be used in candle magic. There are many different types of herbs available, and each one has a specific use; they can also be used with other herbs and oils.

CANDLE

In candle magic, humans discovered the ability to control light. Using candles to symbolize ourselves and our beliefs means we have access to a power beyond ourselves. Candle magic also forms an effective backup for most other forms of magical working.

KNOT

Knot magic works partly with the principle of binding, a type of bidding spell, and also with that of weaving, which was traditionally a female intuitive occupation. It utilizes ribbon, yarn, or anything that can be knotted or braided to signify our aspiration. It is a type of representational magic, and is used with many of the other forms. The techniques of color, form and energies are all used here.

REPRESENTATIONAL

Representational magic involves using an object that represents something or someone for whom you are working the

spell. It helps in concentrating the energy and visualizing the desire and the end result. Representational objects should never be used for negative purposes.

SYMBOLIC

In this system, symbols, rather than objects, are used to represent ideas, people or goals. The symbols can be personal, or such things as Tarot cards, Runes, Hebrew letters or numerology. You may use symbolic magic in your magical workings, and will soon develop your own preferred symbols.

TALISMANS, AMULETS AND CHARMS

These devices use all the other forms of magic in their formation, but principally representational and symbolic magic. They are "charged" (given power) magically, and are usually worn around the neck as jewelery, or carried in a pouch, and incorporate herbs or other objects.

CANDLES

Choose candles carefully with regard to type and color, depending on the purpose of the spell. It is best to use your intuition when choosing the type of candle; for reference, below is a list of the principal types.

Table

These are ideal for many of the spells in this book. They can burn for six to eight hours,

and should be secured in candlesticks. All colors can be used, but they should not be dipped, except in exceptional circumstances, and should be of the best quality possible.

Pillar

This freestanding candle is usually in the form of a simple pillar, although it can be made in other shapes—for example, a heart shape for love spells. It is ideally burned on a flat holder, since it takes some time to burn down.

Taper

Tapers are tall and thin, and need a particularly stable candleholder. They are made either in a mold or by the traditional method of dipping a length of wick into molten white or colored wax. For magical purposes, they should be colored all the way through. They can be used when a quick result is required. Because they are quite fragile, you need to be careful not to break them when anointing them.

Tea lights

Tea lights are excellent when a candle must be left to burn out, but they're less easy to anoint with oils. Poured in small metal pots like small votives, they are normally used in oil burners or specially made holders. They burn for about four hours.

Votive

This candle is designed as an offering, to carry prayers to whichever deity you honor. As the wax melts, the holder, which is made of glass, can become hot so be careful. They are designed to be long-burning, usually lasting between one and seven days.

CHOOSING YOUR CANDLES

There are several things you need to remember when choosing a candle:

1. Candles used for magic should always be virgin (unused) at the start of the working, unless you have deliberately cleared them of past influences. Using candles that have been previously lit can have a detrimental effect on your spell.

2. Charge your candle before using it. This can be done by anointing it with oils associated with the magic you intend to perform, or by simply touching it and filling it with your own energy.

3. The oils used to anoint your candle should be natural fragrances. While charging the candle, smooth from top to bottom when drawing energy toward you, bottom to top when sending energy outwards. For altar use, anoint from the middle to the top and from the middle to the bottom to signify the union of spiritual and physical realms.

4. Consider making your own candles for magical use. It is an art in itself—you infuse candles with your own energy, and thus increase the power of the candle. Oils and colors can be added for extra potency.

DRESSING AND CHARGING CANDLES

Dressing a candle performs two functions. By anointing it with oil you ensure that it burns safely; you can also infuse it with a vibration. Charging a candle ensures you fix the intent of your magical working, and dedicates the candle to its purpose.

Dressing Candles

Any oil can be used for dressing a candle but initially it is best to use either your favorite essential oil, such as frankincense, or an oil infused with an herb appropriate to the task. A list of oils suitable for various purposes is given on pages 38-43.

If you remember that working from the top down draws in power from spiritual sources, and working from the bottom up draws in energy from the earth, it is easy to work correctly for your purpose. Never rub the candle using a back-and-forth movement; you will end up with a confusion of energies, as well as a sputtering candle.

You will need

• Candle
• Oil

Method

Sit quietly and, holding the candle, think carefully about your intent. If you have learned to meditate, enter a meditative state and allow the energies to build up.

To bring something to you, rub oil on the candle in a downward motion from the top to the middle, and then from the bottom to the middle. To send something away from you, rub the oil from the middle of the candle out toward the ends.

Continue with either movement until you have a sense that you have done enough. If you have any oil left on your hands, either rub your hands together until the oil is absorbed or dab the remaining oil from your fingers onto the center of your forehead, which is the Third Eye and the seat of vision. Then say the following or something similar:

I cleanse and consecrate this candle (in the name of your preferred deity if you choose to use one).

May it burn with strength in the service of the Greater Good.

Your candle is now ready for use.

Charging Candles

This is a quick method of more fully charging a candle. This method can be used without having to set up your altar completely. It can also be used to charge your altar candles.

You will need
- A candle or candles of the appropriate color (if you like, mark them with symbols)
- A candleholder
- Matches, rather than a lighter

Method

Hold the candle in your "power hand" (the hand you believe you give out energy with).

Open the other hand and turn that palm toward the sky.

Breathe deeply and visualize your goal.

Now perceive whatever you think of as Universal Energy flowing through the palm that is turned skyward, filling your body.

Visualize that Universal Energy mixing in you with the energy of your intention.

Now allow that mixed energy to flow into the candle.

Be conscious of the energy as it builds up.

Feel the energy streaming into the candle.

Fill it from bottom to top as though the candle were an empty vessel.

If you are comfortable doing so, speak your intention out loud.

As you place the candle in its holder, stabilize the thought in the candle, so it will be converted into pure, clear intent.

Strike a match above the candle.

Bring the flame toward the candle, lighting the wick.

Extinguish the match flame, but do not blow it out in case you blow out the candle.

Stay with the candle for a few moments, visualizing your intention, and feeling its energy moving into the universe.

Leave the area and let the candle burn down as it does its work.

A candle's color, and the symbols inscribed on it, create additional power. As you become more proficient, you will find yourself using certain colors and symbols more often. Try not to be too rigid, and always be open to widening your focus.

CANDLE COLORS

Below is a list of colors and their key associations and purposes. You may not wish to use black candles because of their association with the darker side of magic; if so, consider using dark gray. White can be used if your preferred color is not available.

White
- The Goddess
- Higher Self
- Purity
- Peace
- Virginity

Black
- Binding
- Shape-shifting
- Protection
- Repels negativity

Brown
- Special favors
- To influence friendships
- Healing earth energies

Orange
- General success
- Property deals
- Legal matters
- Justice
- Selling

Purple
- Third eye
- Psychic ability
- Hidden knowledge
- To influence people in high places
- Spiritual power

Blue
- The Element of Water
- Wisdom
- Protection
- Calm
- Good fortune
- Opening communication
- Spiritual inspiration

Pink
- Affection
- Romance
- Caring
- Nurturing
- Care for the planet Earth

Green

- The Element of Earth
- Physical healing
- Monetary success
- Mother Earth
- Tree and plant magic
- Growth
- Personal goals

Red

- The Element of Fire
- Passion
- Strength
- Fast action
- Career goals
- Lust
- Driving force
- Survival

Silver

- The Moon Goddess
- Astral energy
- Female power
- Telepathy
- Clairvoyance
- Intuition
- Dreams

Copper

- Professional growth
- Business productivity
- Career moves
- Passion
- Money goals

Gold

- The Sun God
- Promotes winning
- Male power
- Happiness

Yellow

- The Element of Air
- Intelligence
- The Sun
- Memory
- Imagination supported by logic
- Accelerating learning
- Clearing mental blocks

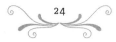

HERBS

Most magical practices make use of herbs. They are often used in incense or oils, and create a type of force field that intensifies the vibration. When the practitioner calls on the power of the gods and spirits, herbs can become even more effective.

The uses of herbs

Protection
Some herbs guard against physical and psychic attacks, injury, accidents and such things as wicked spirits. They usually offer protection in a general way.

Love
These herbs can help you meet new people, overcome shyness and let others know you're open to new relationships. They put out a particular vibration so that those who are interested will answer the call.

Luck
Luck is simply being in the right place at the right time and being able to act on instinct. Luck herbs help you create your own good fortune.

Money
Certain herbs create an environment in which things can happen. They enable the creation of the means to fulfill your needs—perhaps a gift, a raise, or other good fortune.

The A–Z of Magical Plants

ALOE is feminine and ruled by the Moon. Its Element is Water. Its magical properties are protection, success and peace. Aloe has healing qualities, and is used to treat wounds and maintain healthy skin. It also helps combat a variety of bacteria.

AMARANTH (cockscomb) is feminine and ruled by Saturn. Its Element is Fire. When used magically, it is said to repair a broken heart, therefore, it would be useful in certain love spells and rituals. Formerly, it was reputed to bestow invisibility.

ANGELICA is a masculine plant ruled by Venus. Its Element is Fire. It is particularly useful when dealing with protection and exorcism; the root can be carried as an amulet, and the dried leaves can be burned during exorcism rituals.

ANISE is masculine and ruled by the Moon or Jupiter. Its Element is Air. Its magical properties are useful in protection and purification spells. It brings awareness and joy.

APPLE is feminine and ruled by Venus. Its Element is Water. It is used most effectively in the making of magical wands, in love spells and in good-luck charms.

ASH is masculine and ruled by the Sun. Its Element is Water. It is protective, and is often used for making brooms for cleansing, and wands for healing. If the leaves are put under a pillow, they help to induce intuitive dreams. The leaves also bring luck and good fortune when worn.

BALM OF GILEAD is feminine and ruled by Saturn. Its Element is Water. The buds are carried to ease a broken heart, and can be added to love and protection charms and spells.

BASIL, one of the most masculine plants, is ruled by Mars and has Fire as its Element. It is protective, good for love, and is said to promote wealth and business success. It is also useful for healing relationships and for assuring genuineness in a partner.

BAY LAUREL is a masculine plant ruled by the Sun and the Element of Fire. It promotes wisdom and is also a protector, bringing to the fore the ability to develop psychic powers. It finds and forces out negative energy.

BENZOIN is a masculine plant that the Sun rules, along with the Element of Air. A good purifier and preservative, it is used widely in purification incenses.

BETONY is masculine and is ruled by Jupiter and the Element of Fire. Its magical properties are protection and purification. It can be added to incense for this purpose, or stuffed in a pillow to prevent nightmares.

CARAWAY is a masculine plant and is ruled by Mercury. Its Element is Air. Its magical properties are protection and passion. When added to love sachets and charms, it attracts a lover in the physical aspect.

CARNATION is masculine and is ruled by the Sun. Its Element is Fire. Traditionally, it was worn by witches for protection during times of persecution. It adds energy and power when used as an incense during a spell or ritual.

CATNIP is feminine and is ruled by Venus. Its Element is Water. Its magical properties are connected with cat magic, familiars, joy, friendship and love. As an incense, it may be used to consecrate magical tools.

CHAMOMILE is masculine, and is ruled by the Sun or Venus. Its Element is Water. Its magical properties show that it is good as a meditation incense, for centering and creating an atmosphere of peace. Sprinkle it in your home for protection, healing and money. Plant chamomile in your garden to be the guardian of the land, and you will be assured of success. It is an excellent calming herb.

CELANDINE is masculine and is ruled by the Sun. Its Element is Fire. When worn as an amulet, it helps the wearer escape unfair imprisonment or entrapment.

CINQUEFOIL is masculine and is ruled by Jupiter. Its Element is Earth. Hang it around doors and windows to protect you from evil. It is used in spells and charms for prosperity, purification and protection.

CINNAMON is masculine and is ruled by the Sun. Its Element is Fire. Its magical properties are used to help in spiritual quests, augmenting power, love, success, psychic work, healing and cleansing. It is used in incense for healing, clairvoyance and high spiritual vibrations; it is also reputed to be a male aphrodisiac. Use it in prosperity charms. It is an excellent aromatic and makes a good anointing oil for any magical working.

CLOVE is masculine and is ruled by the Sun. Its Element is Fire. Wear it in an amulet or charm to dispel negativity and bind those who speak ill of you. Cloves strung on a red thread can be worn as a protective charm. It helps with money matters, visions, cleansing and purification.

CLOVER is masculine and is ruled by Mercury; it is also associated with the Triple Goddess. Its Element is Air. Use it in rituals for beauty, healing and calming. A four-leaf clover is said to enable one to see fairies, and is considered a general good-luck charm.

COMFREY is a feminine plant and is ruled by Saturn. Its Element is Water. It is useful for travel, money spells and healing. It also honors the Crone aspect of the Goddess.

CORIANDER is masculine and is ruled by Mars and the Element Fire. It is a protector of the home, and is useful in the promotion of peace. It is also helpful in love spells.

COWSLIP is feminine, ruled by Venus with its Element Water. Said to bring luck in love, it also induces contact with departed loved ones in dreams. Someone who washes their face with milk infused with cowslip will draw their beloved closer to them.

CYPRESS is masculine and is ruled by Saturn and its Element, Earth. It is connected with death. Often used to consecrate ritual tools, cypress also has preservative qualities.

DAISY is feminine and is ruled by Venus and the Element, Water. If you decorate your house with it on Midsummer's Eve, it will bring happiness into the home. Daisies are also worn at Midsummer for luck and blessings. Long ago, young women would weave daisy chains and wear them in their hair to attract their beloved.

DANDELION is a masculine plant and is ruled by Jupiter and the Element Air. It is useful for divination and communication.

DILL is masculine and is ruled by Mercury. Its Element is Fire. It is useful in love charms. Dill may also be hung in children's rooms to protect them against evil spirits or bad dreams.

DRAGON'S BLOOD is masculine, and is ruled by Mars with the Element Fire. A type of palm, it is widely included in love, protection and purification spells, usually in the form of a resin. It is carried for good luck; a piece of the plant kept under the bed is said to help alleviate impotency. Dragon's blood increases the potency of other incense too.

ELDER is a feminine plant ruled by Venus and the Element Air. Its branches are widely used for magical wands, and it is considered bad luck to burn it. Its leaves, when hung around doors and windows, are said to ward off evil.

ELECAMPANE is a masculine plant ruled by Mercury and the Element Earth. It is a good aid for meditation and for requesting the presence of spirits.

EUCALYPTUS is feminine and ruled by the Moon and the Element Air. It is used in healing rituals, charms and amulets. If the leaves are put around a blue candle and burned in a room, it can help increase healing energies.

EYEBRIGHT is masculine and ruled by the Sun. Its Element is Air. Traditionally, the plant was said to induce clairvoyant visions and dreams.

FENNEL is masculine and is ruled by Mercury. Its Element is Fire. Including the seeds in money charms is said to bring prosperity and ward off evil spirits. The plant itself is used for purification and protection.

FERN is feminine and is ruled by the planet Saturn and the Element Earth. It is a powerful protector and, if grown near your home, will ward off negativity.

FRANKINCENSE is a masculine herb under the rulership of the Sun and therefore the Element Fire. A purifier of ritual spaces, it is probably the most powerful aid to meditation.

GARDENIA is feminine and ruled by the Moon with its Element, Water. Used extensively in Moon incenses, it attracts good spirits to rituals and enhances love vibrations.

GARLIC is a masculine herb ruled by the planet Mars and consequently the Element Fire. It protects, and is a useful healer and promoter of courage.

GINGER is a masculine herb ruled by Mars and Fire. It encourages power and success, especially in love and financial dealings. It is also a good base for spells because it enhances the vibration.

GINSENG is masculine, ruled by the Sun with the Element of Fire. It aids love and lust, and is considered useful in enhancing beauty. It can also help to create a sense of calm.

HAWTHORN is masculine, ruled by Mars and the Element of Fire. It is used in protective sachets. It is said to promote happiness in marriage and other relationships.

HAZEL is masculine and ruled by the Sun and the Element Air. It is a good wood for magical wands, and is the only one that should be used for divining. It also promotes good luck, particularly when it is bound by red and gold thread.

HEARTSEASE is feminine, ruled by Saturn and the Element Water. It is actually a wild pansy, and can be used with other herbs to ease heartache.

HOLLY is masculine and ruled by Mars; its Element is Fire. When planted around the home, it protects against evil. Holly water is said to protect babies, and when thrown at wild animals it calms them down. The leaves and berries can be carried as an amulet by a man to heighten his virility, enabling him to attract a lover.

HONEYSUCKLE is feminine and ruled by Jupiter and its Element Earth. Planted outside the home, it brings good luck. It is also used in prosperity spells and love charms, and to heighten psychic ability.

HOPS, a masculine plant ruled by Mars and the Element Water, can be used in healing and to promote sleep.

HYSSOP is masculine. Its ruler is Jupiter and its Element is Fire. The plant was widely used during the Middle Ages for purification, cleansing and consecration rituals. Use it in purification baths, and for protective and banishing spells. Hyssop works best in the form of an essential oil in incense.

IVY is a masculine plant ruled by Saturn, and its Element is Water. It protects the houses it grows on from evil and harm. In the old traditions, ivy and holly were given to newlyweds as good-luck charms.

JASMINE is feminine and is ruled by Jupiter and the Element Earth. It was historically used by women to attract men.

JUNIPER is a masculine plant ruled by the Sun, and its Element is Fire. It helps protect

against accidents, harm and theft. Once they have been dried and worn as a charm, juniper berries are used to attract lovers. The herb also breaks hexes and curses.

LAVENDER is a masculine plant ruled by Mercury and the Element of Air. It is one of the most useful herbs, and can be used for healing, and promoting good wishes and sleep; it can also be used to attract men.

LEMON BALM is feminine, and is ruled by the Moon or Neptune. Its Element is Water. It is said to be an aphrodisiac, and helps ease heartache at the end of a relationship.

LEMON VERBENA is feminine, ruled by Venus and the Element Air. It is used in love charms to promote attractiveness. Wear it around your neck or place it under a pillow to help prevent bad dreams. It is also said to help heal wounds.

LILAC is a feminine plant that is ruled by the planet Venus. Its Element is Air. It is a good protector that also banishes evil.

LINDEN is feminine, ruled by Jupiter, and its Element is Water. It is said to be the tree of immortality, and is associated with conjugal love or attraction and longevity. It is supposed to help prevent intoxication.

LOVAGE is masculine, ruled by the Sun. Its Element is Water. The dried and powdered root should be added to cleansing and purification baths to release negativity. Carry it to attract a lover. Also carry it when meeting new people.

MANDRAKE is a masculine plant ruled by Mercury and the Element Earth. It is very useful in incense for increasing the sex drive (both male and female) and is best used prior to the Full Moon.

MARIGOLD is masculine, and is ruled by the Sun. Its Element is Fire. Prophecy, legal matters, the psyche, seeing magical creatures, love, divination dreams, business or legal affairs and renewing personal energy are all assisted by marigold. It is good for finding someone who has done you wrong. It is sometimes added to love sachets. It should be gathered at noon.

MARJORAM is masculine and is ruled by Mercury with the Element Air. It protects against evil and promotes love and healing; it is also helpful to those who are grieving.

MEADOWSWEET is feminine, its planet is Jupiter, and it is ruled by Water. It is a sacred herb of the Druids, and gives protection against evil; it also promotes love, balance and harmony. Place meadowsweet on your altar when making love charms and conducting love spells to increase their potency. It can be worn at Lammas to join with the Goddess.

MINT is a masculine plant ruled by Mercury or Venus, and has the Element Air. It promotes healing and the ability to gain money, and is useful for successful travel. It can aid digestion, and calms the emotions.

MUGWORT, a feminine plant, is ruled by Venus and the Element Air. It is probably the most widely used herb by witches, and promotes psychic ability and prophetic dreams. It is good for astral projection.

MULLEIN is a masculine plant ruled by Saturn, and has the Element of Fire. This is used for courage, and for protection from wild animals and evil spirits. It is also used for cleansing and purifying ritual tools and altars, and the cleansing of psychic places and sacred spaces before and after working. It guards against nightmares, and can be substituted for graveyard dust.

MYRRH is a feminine plant ruled by the Moon or Jupiter and the Element Water. It is purifying and protective, and is especially useful when used with frankincense.

MYRTLE is feminine, ruled by Venus, and its Element is Water. Myrtle was sacred to the Greek goddess Venus and has been used in love charms and spells throughout history. It should be grown indoors for good luck. Carry or wear myrtle leaves to attract love; charms made of the wood have special magical properties. Wear fresh myrtle leaves while making love charms, potions or during rituals for love, and include it in them.

NETTLE is a masculine plant ruled by Mars, and its Element is Fire. It helps guard against danger, and promotes courage.

NUTMEG is feminine, ruled by Jupiter, and its Element is Air. It helps promote clairvoyance and psychic powers. When used with green candles, it aids prosperity.

OAK is masculine, and is ruled by the Sun and the Element Fire. It is often employed by witches and used in power wands. It also protects against evil spirits, and can be used to promote a better sex life.

ORANGE is a feminine plant ruled by Jupiter and the Element Water. It is used as a love charm; in the East it is used for good luck.

ORRIS ROOT is a feminine plant, ruled by Venus and has the Element Water. The powder is used as a love-drawing herb and to increase sexual appeal. Used in charms, amulets, sachets, incenses and baths, it will also protect you. Hung on a cord, it can act as a pendulum.

PARSLEY is a masculine herb ruled by Mercury and Air. It wards off evil, and is a useful aid to those who drink too much.

Parsley may be used in purification baths and as a way to ward off misfortune.

PATCHOULI is a feminine plant that is ruled by Saturn; its Element is Earth. The plant is an aphrodisiac and helps attract lovers. It can be substituted for graveyard dust. Use it with green candles to ensure prosperity. Sprinkle it on money to spread your wealth.

PENNYROYAL is a masculine plant ruled by Mars; its Element is Fire. It is used for protection and, because it prevents weariness during long journeys, it is often carried on ships. Pennyroyal is also an insect deterrent. It should be avoided while pregnant.

PEPPER (black) is a masculine plant that is ruled by Mars with its Element of Fire; it can be used in protective charms against the evil eye. Mixed with salt, it dispels evil, which may be why it is also used on food.

PIMPERNEL is a masculine plant that is ruled by Mercury and has the Element Air. You should wear it to keep people from deceiving you. It is said to help ward off ill health and accidents. The juice is used to purify and empower ritual weapons.

PINE is masculine and ruled by Mars; it has the Element Air. It helps you focus and, if burned, will help cleanse the atmosphere. Its sawdust is often used as a base for incense, particularly in those associated with money.

POPPY is feminine, ruled by the Moon, and has the Element Water. Poppy seeds can be used in love sachets; carry them or a dried seed pod as a prosperity charm.

ROSE is a feminine plant ruled by Venus and the Element Water. It is perhaps the most widely used plant in love and good-luck workings. Roses are also added to "fast luck" mixtures designed to make things happen quickly. It is also a good calming agent when situations become difficult.

ROSEMARY is a masculine plant ruled by the Sun and the Element of Fire. It helps promote memory and sleep; it is an excellent purifier. It should be used to cleanse your hands before performing magic or rituals. You can hang it in doorways to deter thieves.

ROWAN is a masculine plant ruled by the Sun and the Element Fire. Rowan wood is used for divining rods and wands; its leaves and bark are used in divination rituals. It is also used for protection, good luck and healing. When two twigs are tied together to form a cross, it is a protective device.

RUE is masculine, ruled by the Sun and the Element Fire. Protective when hung by a door, it can break hexes by sending the negativity back from where it came. It is good

for clearing the mind of emotional clutter, and purifying ritual spaces and tools.

SAFFRON is masculine, ruled by the Sun and the Element Fire. It was used in rituals to honor the Goddess of the Moon, Ashtoreth. It dispels melancholy and restores sexual prowess in men. It is used to cleanse the hands in healing processes, and is also used in prosperity incenses.

SAGE is masculine, ruled by either Jupiter or Venus and the Element Air. It promotes financial gain and good wishes; it is also a good healer and protector.

ST. JOHN'S WORT is a masculine plant ruled by the Sun and the Element of Fire. It helps protect against bad dreams and encourages the willpower to do something difficult.

SANDALWOOD is feminine, ruled by the Moon, and its Element is Air. It has high spiritual vibrations, so should be mixed with frankincense and burned at the time of the Full Moon. Anything visualized at this time is said to come true. It also clears negativity, so is good for purification, protection and healings.

SUNFLOWER is masculine and is ruled by the Sun and the Element of Fire. It is extremely useful, for the plant allows you to discover the truth if you sleep with it under your bed. It is said to guard the garden against marauders and pests.

THYME is a feminine herb that is ruled by the planet Venus and the Element Water. It is a good guardian against negative energy and an extremely good cleanser if combined with marjoram. It helps promote psychic powers, and it is said to make women irresistible.

VALERIAN is feminine and is ruled by Venus and the Element Water. It is said to enhance sleep; it also promotes love and rids your house of evil. It is also said to protect against lightning.

VANILLA is feminine, ruled by Venus, and its Element is Water. The bean is used in love charms, while the oil is worn as an aphrodisiac. Mix it with sugar to make infusions for love.

VERVAIN is feminine and is ruled by Venus with the Element Earth. Good for the ritual cleansing of sacred space, magical cleansing baths and purification incenses, it should be hung over the bed to prevent nightmares. Vervain is also excellent for use in prosperity charms and spells as it brings good luck and inspiration. It should be picked before sunrise. While it is said to control sexual urges (supposedly for seven years), it is also used in love and protection charms, presumably to ensure fidelity.

VIOLET is feminine, ruled by Venus, and its Element is Water. It brings changes in luck or fortune. Mix with lavender for a powerful love charm. A violet and lavender compress is said to help soothe headaches. The scent will clear the mind and relax the wearer, and the flowers can be carried as a good-luck charm.

WALNUT is masculine, ruled by the Sun, and the Element is Fire. Carry the nut as a charm to strengthen the heart. It is said to attract lightning.

WILLOW is feminine and ruled by the Moon. The Element is Water. Willow wands can be used for healing and are at their strongest when used at the New Moon. Willow guards against evil, and this is where the expression "knock on wood" comes from.

WITCH HAZEL is masculine, ruled by the Sun, with the Element Fire. The wood is used to make divining rods. Witch hazel gives protection and promotes fidelity, healing the heart. It cools all the passions.

WORMWOOD is masculine, ruled by Mars, with the Element Air. Wormwood is poisonous, but is sometimes burned in smudge sticks to gain protection from wandering spirits. It is said that it enables the dead to be released from this plane so they may find peace. It is also used in divinatory and clairvoyance incenses,

initiation rites and tests of courage. Mixed with sandalwood, it summons spirits.

YARROW is feminine and ruled by Venus. Its Element is Water. It is said that yarrow was once a component in incense used for incantations. It is powerful in divination and love spells too. It exorcises evil, dispels negativity, and enhances psychic ability and divination. Yarrow tea, drunk prior to divination, will enhance powers of perception; a touch of peppermint enhances the action of this brew. The plant is also traditionally used in courage, love and marriage charms.

YUCCA is masculine, and ruled by Mars. Its Element is Fire. Yucca is said to help with shape-shifting. If a strand of a leaf is tied around one's head, and an animal is visualized, the wearer takes on the qualities of that animal. Yucca is used to purify the body before performing magic. A cross formed from yucca leaves is said to protect the hearth, the center of the home.

Making an Herb Bundle
With any spiritual intent, wash and cleanse yourself—getting rid of any negative energy in the process—before you begin. There are a few other guidelines you'll need to follow.

• Before picking a plant, honor the plant and ask its permission to take a branch or stem for your spiritual intent. When picking

stems, make sure they are long enough to be bound together.

• Use any of the herbs mentioned above, or use pine or cypress.

• If you want to, add essential oils, but use them sparingly and try to choose one that will enhance the purpose of, or add an extra quality to, your bundle.

You will need
• Selection of leaves and stems
• Rubber band
• Thick cotton string
• Small bowl

Method
Arrange a handful of leaves and stems fairly symmetrically into a bundle—don't use too many.

Put the stems in the rubber band to keep the pieces together while you tie the bundle, then remove it when you have finished.

Take a long piece of thick cotton string and place the bundle top (the thicker end) in the middle of it.

Bind the bundle together tightly in a criss-cross fashion, starting at the top and finishing at the bottom of the stems. (Take your time with this—the more secure you make the bundle, the better it will burn. Some leaves or twigs may protrude, so use a receptacle to catch falling ashes.)

Bind the end of your bundle securely with the string, and perhaps make a dedication to your purpose.

You will have a cone-shaped bundle. Let it dry completely before burning; it won't burn properly if it is at all damp or green.

Light the thick top end, then blow the flame out so it smolders. Some pieces may drop out of the bundle, so have a bowl or receptacle handy to catch them.

Herb bundles are moved to where the fragrant smoke is needed. In rituals, you would use the cardinal points. Walk around slowly, wafting the smoke into the corners of the room. (You may have to keep blowing on the lit end to keep it burning.) As you blow, remember that you are using the principle of Air. You can also direct the smoke with your hands, a branch, or even a special stone. Amber can also be used; it's especially appropriate, as it is a resin from a plant. This action should get rid of any negative vibrations while energizing the protective frequencies.

If you want to cleanse the energy of a friend (or yourself), waft the smoke all around the body, starting at the head and gradually moving down to the feet. Move in a clockwise direction, because this creates positivity. You can direct the smoke with your hand or a feather, or whatever feels good to you. A seashell is good, since it represents the Goddess. You can also chant or sing. Whatever you do, do it with a pure mind and spirit. When you have finished, keep the bundle safe until it has extinguished itself, and then open a window to clear the space.

Decorative bundles

If you don't intend to burn the bundle, there are many other possibilities. Bundles can be bound with color, feeling and meaning. Oils will add energy and aroma. You can use spices, fruits, fragrant wood, minerals, resins or flowers. Depending on how you plan to display the bundle, you can use pretty much anything that has meaning and fragrance.

OILS

At various points in this book, you will read about oils that can be used as adjuncts to magic. They are an easy way of using plants in magical workings.

Below are some oils that should be part of every magical practitioner's way of working. For your reference, their Latin names are also given. All of them are easy to find, and even though the initial expense may seem prohibitive, if they are stored according to directions, they will last for some time.

CINNAMON *(Cinnamomum zeylanicum)*, with its warm vibration, brings into our hearts love from higher realms, if only we allow it. The warm glow of cinnamon drifts through space and time, transforming sadness into happiness.

CLARY SAGE *(Salvia sclarea)* has benefits for both the physical and mental aspects of humankind, teaching us to be content with what we have. It brings prosperity of the spirit, and the realization that most problems arise in our imagination. This herb lifts the spirit and links us with eternal wisdom.

FRANKINCENSE *(Boswellia carterii)*, also called olibanum, holds some of the wisdom of the universe, both spiritual and meditative. Able to cleanse most negative influences, it acts as a spiritual prop. It works beyond the auric field, affecting the subtle realms of energy and adapting the spiritual state.

GERANIUM *(Pelargonium graveolens)* resonates with Mother Earth and all that is feminine. It typifies the energy of Goddess culture. Its energy is transformational, and must be used with respect. It comforts our pain and opens our hearts.

JASMINE *(Jasminum officinale)* provides us with our personal sanctuary and allows us access to a greater understanding of the spirit. It is said that jasmine brings the angelic kingdom within our reach, thus allowing us to be the best we can. It gives understanding and acceptance of the true meaning of spirituality.

LAVENDER *(Lavendula augustifolia)* is caring and nurturing. By allowing the heavenly energies close to the physical, it brings about healing and signifies the

protective love of Mother Earth. Gentle and relaxing, it changes the perception to enable one to make progress. Lavender will not allow negative emotion to remain present within the aura for long.

MYRRH (*Commiphora myrrha*) signifies the pathway of the soul, allowing us to let go when the time is right. Wounds of body, mind and spirit are healed by myrrh, and it brings the realization that we no longer need to carry our burdens, releasing them from deep within. When combined with other oils, it enhances—and is enhanced by—them.

NEROLI (*Citrus aurantium*) is one of the most precious essential oils, its vibration being one of the highest. It is pure spirit, and is loving and peaceful. It brings self-recognition and respite because it allows development of a new perspective, helping us to cast off the bonds of old ways of relating and develop unconditional love. In magical working, it allows one to be a pure channel.

NUTMEG (*Myristica fragrans*) helps us reconnect with the higher realms of spirit and experience a sense of spiritual wonderment. When the spirit is affected by disappointment, spiritual pain and displacement, nutmeg brings hopes, dreams and prayers back into focus.

ROSE ABSOLUT (*Rosa centifolia*) In India, the "Great Mother" was known as the "Holy Rose," and this personification reveals just how profound the effects of this perfume are when used magically. Said to be the perfume of the guardians or messengers who guide us in times of need, it is a soul fragrance that allows us to access divine mysteries. It is associated with the true needs of the heart.

ROSEMARY (*Rosmarinus officinalis*) reminds us of our purpose and our spiritual journey. It opens the human spirit to understanding and wisdom, and encourages confidence and clarity of purpose. It cleanses the aura and enables us to assist others in their search for spirituality.

SANDALWOOD (*Santalum album*) acts as a bridge between heaven and earth, and allows us to make contact with divine beings. It enables us to be calm enough to hear the music of the spheres, and brings us into balance with the Cosmos. It clarifies our strength of conviction.

YLANG YLANG (*Cananga odorata*) gives a new appreciation of the sensual side of our being. It balances the spirit so we can be open to pleasures of the physical realm while still appreciating spiritual passions. It brings a sense of completion to tasks that belong to the physical realm. Used magically, it achieves a balanced manifestation.

Ritual Bathing

Purification baths are not about personal cleanliness, they are part of acknowledging that the power and energy will flow more freely through a cleansed "vessel." There is a method for a ritual bath here, as well as a way of preparing bath salts.

Essential oils contain all of the Elements. They are products of the Earth, having been distilled; they flow (Water); they will burn (Fire); and they release perfume (Air). When the water and salt of a ritual bath are combined, we have a perfect vehicle for cleansing our subtle energies.

Ritual Bath Oil Blends

- Neroli 3 drops
- Orange 1 drop
- Petitgrain 2 drops
- Myrtle 3 drops
- Clary sage 1 drop
- Lemon 1 drop
- Rosemary 2 drops
- Eucalyptus 1 drop
- Lavender 3 drops
- Chamomile 3 drops
- Mandarin 3 drops
- Frankincense 4 drops
- Lemon 2 drops
- Rose 3 drops
- Neroli 3 drops

Essential Oil Blends

The following blends can be used for anointing candles and for blessing objects as well as for personal use. Ideally, when you combine oils, they should be shaken together and left for at least an hour so that the synergy begins to work.

Pure essential oils should never be ingested or used directly on the skin. If you intend to use them as massage oils, make sure to use a carrier oil such as almond or grapeseed.

Romance Magnet Oil

- 2 drops ylang ylang oil
- 2 drops sandalwood oil
- 2 drops clary sage oil

To attract love, rub romance magnet oil onto a pink candle, then burn it for three hours a day, every day, until the person makes an advance. The candle should be snuffed rather than blown out.

Lover's Oil

- 5 drops rosewood oil
- 5 drops rosemary oil
- 3 drops tangerine oil
- 3 drops lemon oil

Lover's oil may be used to enhance a relationship in all sorts of ways. Consecrate a candle with lover's oil and light it half an hour before your date arrives.

Marriage Oil

- 2 drops frankincense oil
- 3 drops cypress oil
- 2 drops sandalwood oil

This oil is used to reinforce a marriage

relationship, regardless of whether the union is good. It may also be used to help steer a relationship toward commitment. Simply burn a pink or lilac-colored candle anointed with marriage oil when you and your partner are together.

Desire Oil

- 3 drops lavender oil
- 3 drops orange oil
- 1 drop lemon oil

Desire oil is meant to entice another person. If someone just needs a little prompting, a red, orange, pink, blue or white candle should be anointed and lit when the two of you are together. If the person doesn't respond, speak their name as you light a candle blessed with this oil. Allow the candles to burn for two hours, then snuff them out. Repeat each night until the person reacts.

Dream Potion

- 10 drops jasmine oil
- 10 drops nutmeg oil
- 3 drops clary sage

This oil can be used to enhance the atmosphere of the bedroom before sleep. It is best burned in an aromatherapy lamp rather than used as a body oil.

To Strengthen an Existing Relationship

- 10 drops rose oil
- 10 drops sandalwood oil

- 5 drops lavender oil

This oil can be used as a perfume or to scent the atmosphere.

Aphrodisiac Oil

Use as a perfume or add to 50ml (2 fl oz) of unscented massage oil (such as grapeseed or almond oil), and have fun!

- 10 drops ylang ylang
- 2 drops cinnamon
- 5 drops sweet orange
- 3 drops jasmine oil
- 10 drops patchouli
- 10 drops sandalwood

Oils for Ritual Work

These blends can be used in ritual work.

Sacred Space Blend

- 20 drops juniper berry oil
- 10 drops frankincense oil
- 10 drops sandalwood oil
- 5 drops rosemary oil
- 2 drops nutmeg oil

This is a good blend to use when you need to create a sacred space or magical circle.

Prosperity Blend

- Equal parts patchouli and basil oil

This combination creates the right vibration for prosperity of all sorts (not just financial).

Altar Oil Blend

- 4 parts frankincense

- 3 parts myrrh
- 1 part galangal
- 1 part vervain
- 1 part lavender

This blend can be used to anoint your altar, if you use one, or around your sacred space at regular intervals, before you undertake any ritual, to purify and empower the space.

Goddess Oil Blend

- 10 drops neroli oil
- 5 drops nutmeg oil
- 10 drops sandalwood oil
- 10 drops jasmine oil

When you invoke the Goddess, this oil is wonderful for allowing your vibration to meet with hers at any time of the year.

Protection Blend

- 10 drops juniper oil
- 5 drops vetiver oil
- 5 drops basil oil
- 2 drops clove oil

If you feel in need of protection, this oil can be used in an aromatherapy burner or sprinkled on a tissue and placed on a warm radiator.

Using Essential Oils in the Auric Field

When they begin working magically, most practitioners find that they become more sensitive to the vibrations of the everyday world. Others' vibrations can be hard to deal with. This difficulty arises because your own "force field," or aura—which you

carry with you always—begins to vibrate at a different level than the one to which you were accustomed.

If you begin to do a great deal of magical work, you must learn to protect yourself, perhaps from onslaughts of negativity or subtle vibrations over which others have no control. Remember that you have at your disposal the means for control, and it should become a regular part of your routine to enhance your own aura and to protect that of others. Essential oils can help you do this.

Using Oils for Protective Purposes

Method 1

Put one drop of pure, undiluted essential oil in the center of your palm and rub your hands together. Holding your hands about 4in (10cm) away from your body, smooth around the outside of this space, from the top of your head down to your feet and then back up again. Make sure you have covered every part that you can reach of this subtle body. This is also known as protecting your aura.

Method 2

Use your oils in a spray bottle or diffuser, spraying around your body and over the top of your head again. Prepare your oils in advance, and store them for a week in a quiet, dark place away from electrical equipment. On the eighth day, use a new spray bottle, preferably made of glass; add about 25ml (1 fl oz) of pure water to the essential oils, and shake the bottle vigorously. This can also be used to protect your sacred space or immediate environment.

Energizing Oils

The following energizing oils will boost your power (the proportions used can be to your personal preference): Basil, Coriander, Eucalyptus, Fir, Lemon, Peppermint, and Spruce.

Harmonizing Oils

The oils in this group are used for establishing harmony in the person who uses them, and in the atmosphere: Clary sage, Fennel, Geranium, Ginger, Juniper, Lavender, Mandarin, Orange, Petitgrain.

The following recipes are based on these oils:

Cleansing Blend

- Pine 4 drops
- Lemon 3 drops
- Basil 3 drops
- Fir needle 5 drops
- Spruce 5 drops

This blend cleanses the aura, and gives an idea of the correct proportions to use.

Aura Harmonization

- Geranium 4 drops
- Juniper 2 drops
- Orange 6 drops
- Fennel 1 drop
- Petitgrain 6 drops

This blend is particularly useful when you wish to cleanse and harmonize your aura.

Connecting with the Essential

The oils below can help you make a connection with your spiritual self, the essential you: Frankincense, Rose, Neroli, Linden blossom, Jasmine.

Linking Blend

- Galbanum 1 drop
- Frankincense 4 drops
- Jasmine 2 drops
- Neroli 7 drops
- Rose 7 drops

DEITIES AND THEIR WORSHIP

The more accustomed you become to making spells, the more you will begin to appreciate the power of the various deities and how that power is used.

By placing representations of the deities on your altar, or calling on them to assist in your spells, you are accessing an energy that might not otherwise be available to you. You must be comfortable with this, and will therefore use the entities that appeal to you.

Included here are some spells and rituals to give you an idea of how to call upon the gods or use their energies. You may research further, both to learn about gods and goddesses appropriate for your workings, and to find spells that satisfy your creativity.

Gaulish Gods
BELENUS (also Bel) is the God of light and the Sun, also known as the Shining One. The most worshipped Celtic god, he has authority for the welfare of sheep and cattle. The Feast of Beltane means "Fire of Bel."

CERNUNNOS is a god of fertility, life, animals, wealth and the underworld. Usually shown with a stag's antlers, he carries a purse filled with coins. The horned god, he is born at the winter solstice, marries the Goddess of the Moon at Beltane, and dies at the summer solstice. Worshipped in Gaul, he is identified as Herne the Hunter in Britain. With the Goddess of the Moon, he jointly rules over the cycle of life, death and reincarnation.

OGMIOS is the God of scholars and eloquence. Known in Ireland as Ogma, he is a hero god who invented the runic language of the Druids, the Ogham Staves. Associated with the Greek hero Heracles, he is shown as a bald old man dressed in a lion's skin.

SUCELLUS is the guardian of forests and the God of agriculture; he also ferries the dead to the afterlife. He is often portrayed with a huge hammer and a dog by his side. In this aspect, he links with the Norse Thor and the Egyptian Anubis.

TARANIS, "the thunderer," has as his symbols the wheel, representing the

Wheel of Life, and the lightning bolt. He is sometimes identified with the Roman God Jupiter and the Norse God Thor.

TEUTATES is a god of war, fertility and wealth; his name means "the god of the tribe." He was worshipped at a time when human sacrifices were made. The counterpart of the Roman god Mars, he was also known as Alborix, King of the World.

Gaulish Goddesses

BELISAMA is goddess of light and fire, forging and craft; she is the wife of Belenus. She relates to the Roman goddess Minerva, and to the Greek goddess Athena. Her name means "most brilliant."

EPONA is the goddess of horses, mules and the cavalry. She is usually shown lying on a horse, sitting sidesaddle, or standing surrounded by many horses. Her other symbol is that of the cornucopia—the horn of plenty—which suggests that she may also have been a fertility or corn Goddess.

ROSMERTA is a goddess of fertility and wealth. Her stick with two snakes links her to Mercury, messenger of the Roman gods. The cornucopia—another of her symbols—identifies her as a fertility goddess, and thus connects her with Epona.

Irish Gods

BRES is the god of fertility and agriculture. He is the son of Elatha, a prince of the Fomorians, and Eriu, a queen of the Tuatha De Danann.

BILE corresponds with the Gaulish God Belenus, and shares his attributes.

DAGDA (also Dagde, DaGodevas) is God of the Earth and Father-God—that is, the masculine principle. A formidable warrior and skilled craftsman, he has a club that can restore life as well as kill. His symbols are a bottomless cauldron of plenty and a harp with which he rules the seasons.

DIAN CECHT (also Dianchcht) is a god of healing. He rules the waters that restore life to the old and dying gods. When Nuada (king of the Tuatha De Danann) lost his hand in battle, Dian Cecht made him a silver one.

LUGH was worshipped during the thirty-day midsummer feast in Ireland. Magical sexual rites undertaken in his name ensured the ripening of the crops and a prosperous harvest. He is linked with Rosmerta in Gaul, and also corresponds to the Roman god Mercury. His animal totems are the raven and the lynx, representing deviousness. He is known as Lleu in Wales.

NODENS was a god of healing. His magic hounds were said to be able to cure the sick.

Irish Goddesses

AIRMID is a healing goddess and is responsible for medicinal plants. She is the keeper of the spring that brings the dead back to life.

BOANN is a goddess of bounty and fertility whose totem is the sacred white cow. She was the wife of Nechtan, a water deity. One story is that the father of her son was Dagda.

BRIGHID (also Bridget, Brigit, Brighid, Brigindo) is the goddess of healing and fertility, patroness of smiths, poets and doctors. Often symbolized by a white swan or a cow with red horns, she was thought to be the daughter of Dagda. Her festival is that of Imbolc, observed on February 2nd. She shares attributes with the ancient Greek Triple Goddess Hecate.

DANU (also Don in Welsh) probably existed earlier as Anu, the Universal Mother. She is said to be to be the mother of Dagda, God of the Tuatha De Danaan.

MORRIGAN is the goddess of war and death. Married to Dagda, she is linked with negative femininity and the more fearsome characteristics of the Triple Goddess. She could transform into a crow or raven.

TUATHA DE DANANN ("People of the Goddess Danu") are the members of an ancient race that inhabited Ireland before Danu made Dagda, her son, their God. They perfected the use of magic and are credited with the possession of magical powers and great wisdom. The plow, the hazel and the Sun were sacred to them.

Welsh Gods

AMAETHON is the Welsh god of agriculture.

BRAN is a hero god and also the god of poetry and the underworld. His name means "raven."

BELATU-CADROS is a god of war and of the destruction of enemies. His name means "fair shining one." The Romans linked him with Mars.

DEWI is a dragon god, represented by the Great Red Serpent. The official emblem of Wales is derived from this representation.

DYLAN is a sea god, brother of Lleu. He is said to have slipped into the sea at birth, possibly in order to avoid the curses their mother, Arianrhod, placed upon them.

GWYDION is a warrior and a magician god. He was brother to Arianrhod. There are various stories about him; the most well-known suggests that he fathered Lleu and Dylan or that he raised and passed on his knowledge to Lleu.

LLEU (also Lleu Llaw Gyffes) is the god of arts and crafts, as well as a solar and hero god. His name translates as "the fair one has a skillful hand." Brother of Dylan, he was denied a name by his mother, Arianrhod (see below). Overcoming these problems, he became one of the most revered of Welsh gods.

MATH is an eminent magician and lord of North Wales, brother of Don, the Welsh mother-Goddess. Returning from battle, he discovered that his foot-holder, who had to be a virgin, had been raped by his nephews (see Arianrhod). Furious, he turned them first into a stag and a hind, then a boar and a sow, and then a wolf and a she-wolf.

Welsh Goddesses

ARIANRHOD is a Moon goddess. Her name means "silver wheel." She is the daughter of Don, sister of Gwydion. Given the position of foot-holder to Math, and therefore supposedly a virgin, she nevertheless gave birth to Dylan and Lleu, cursing the latter, thus taking her revenge on all men. She is an aspect of the Triple Goddess.

BRANWEN is the goddess of love and beauty. She is linked with the Greek goddess Aphrodite and the Roman goddess Venus.

CERIDWEN is best known in her aspect of the "Dark Goddess." She was the keeper of the Cauldron of Inspiration and Knowledge. She causes things to be reborn (changed, by having been given her protection), and at the same time is in charge of the actual process of generation. She has the power of knowing what is needed, whatever the circumstances.

RHIANNON is believed to be the Welsh counterpart of the Gaulish horse goddess Epona and the Irish goddess Macha.

Egyptian Gods

AMUN (also Ammon, Amon Ra) was a supreme god of the ancient Egyptians. His worship spread to Greece, where he was identified with Zeus, and to Rome, where he was known as Jupiter Ammon.

ANUBIS is the god of mummification and protector of tombs, and is often represented as having a jackal's head. He weighed the souls of the dead against a feather.

ATUM is known as "the complete one." He is a great creator-god thought to have been the oldest worshipped at Heliopolis. He is usually shown wearing a double crown.

APIS, a God depicted as a bull, symbolized fertility and strength in war. Apis was worshipped especially at Memphis.

BES is a protector of women during pregnancy and childbirth. Fond of parties and sensual music, he is also credited with being able to dispel evil spirits.

GEB (also Kebu, Seb, Sibu, Sivu) is a God of the earth, earthquakes and fertility. His sister Nut was his counterpart as the Sky Goddess.

HORUS, a sky god whose symbol is the hawk, is usually depicted as a falcon-headed man. He was regarded as the protector of the monarchy, and his name was often added to royal titles. He assumed various aspects and was known to the Greeks as Harpocrates (Horus the Child).

KHEPHRA (also Khephera, Khopri) is said to have been self-created and God of the Dawn Sun. His symbol is the scarab beetle, which stands for health, strength and virility. Wear a scarab amulet if you wish to invoke Khephra's protection.

KHONSU, whose name means "he who crosses," was a Moon god worshipped especially at Thebes, and was the divine son of Amun and Mut.

OSIRIS, a god originally associated with fertility, was the husband of Isis and father of Horus. He is known chiefly through the story of his death at the hand of his brother Seth, and his subsequent restoration by his wife Isis to a new life as ruler of the Afterlife.

PTAH was an ancient deity of Memphis, creator of the universe, god of artisans and husband of Sekhmet. He became one of the chief deities of Egypt and was identified by the Greeks with Hephaestus.

RA, the supreme Egyptian Sun God, was worshipped as the creator of all life and is often portrayed with a falcon's head bearing the solar disc. He appears traveling in his ship with other gods, crossing the sky by day and journeying through the underworld at the dead of night.

SETH, as one of the oldest of the Egyptian deities, is the god of chaos and evil. He is shown as a man with the head of a monster.

THOTH the God of knowledge, law, wisdom, writing and the Moon, is also the measurer of time and is depicted as an ibis, a man with the head of an ibis, or as a baboon.

Egyptian Goddesses

BAST (also Bastet) is usually shown as a woman with the head of a cat, wearing one gold earring and carrying a sistrum in her right hand. She is the goddess of pleasure, dancing, music and joy. Cats were considered to be her sacred animal, and were therefore protected from harm.

HATHOR is a sky goddess, the patron of love and joy, represented variously as a cow, with a cow's head or ears, or with a solar disk between the cow's horns. Her name means "House of Horus."

ISIS is first a nature Goddess, wife of Osiris and mother of Horus. Her worship spread to Western Asia, Greece and Rome, where she was identified with various local goddesses. When Seth killed Osiris, she sought his scattered body so she could give birth to Horus, a sky god.

MAAT is the goddess of truth, justice and cosmic order, and was the daughter of Ra. She is depicted as a young and beautiful woman, seated or standing, with a feather on her head.

MUT is the queen of all the gods, and is regarded as the wife of all living things. She was also the wife of Amon and mother of Khonsu. She is usually depicted with the head of a vulture. Her name means "the mother."

NUT, the Sky Goddess, was thought to swallow the Sun at night and give birth to it in the morning. She is usually shown as a naked woman with her body arched above the earth, which she touches with her feet and hands.

SEKHMET is a fierce lion goddess, counterpart of the gentler cat goddess Bast and wife of Ptah at Memphis. Her messengers were abominable creatures who could bring about diseases and other curses on humankind.

Greek Gods

APOLLO, son of Zeus and Leto and brother of Artemis, is presented as the ideal type of manly beauty. He is associated with the Sun and linked especially with music, poetic inspiration, archery, medicine and pastoral life.

ASCLEPIUS, as god of healing and the son of Apollo, is often represented wearing a staff with a serpent coiled around it. He sometimes bears a scroll or tablet thought to represent medical learning.

CHAOS is the first created being, from which came the primeval deities Gaia, Tartarus, Erebus and Nyx.

CRONUS (also Kronos) is the leader of the Titans and the ruler of time. He married his sister Rhea, who bore him several children who became Gods, including Zeus, who eventually overthrew him.

DIONYSUS was called Bacchus by the Romans, and was originally a god of the fertility of nature. Associated with wild and ecstatic religious rites, in later traditions he is a god of wine who loosens inhibitions and inspires creativity in music and poetry.

EREBUS is the primeval god of darkness, son of Chaos.

HADES is the God of the Underworld who received as his weapon the helmet of invisibility. He captured Persephone as his consort, causing chaos in the upper world when Demeter went searching for Persephone.

HELIOS is the Sun personified as a god. He is generally represented as a charioteer driving daily from east to west across the sky.

HEPHAESTUS is the god of fire (especially the smithy fire) and was identified with Vulcan by the Romans. He is also the god of craftsmen of all kinds—metalworkers, blacksmiths, leatherworkers, weavers, potters and painters.

HERMES is the messenger of the gods and the god of merchants, thieves and public speaking. Usually pictured as a herald equipped for traveling with broad-brimmed hat, winged shoes and a winged rod, he was identified by the Romans with Mercury.

HYPNOS, the god of sleep, was the son of Nyx (night).

PAN, as a god of flocks and herds, is usually represented with the horns, ears and legs of a goat on a man's body. He was thought of as loving mountains, caves and lonely places as well as playing the pan-pipes. He is also a god of Nature.

Poseidon is the god of the sea, water, earthquakes and horses. When angered, he was perceived as needing to be pacified. He is often portrayed with a trident in his hand and is identified with the Roman god Neptune.

PROTEUS is a minor sea god with the power of prophecy. He would assume different shapes to avoid answering questions.

SILENUS, an ancient woodland deity, was entrusted with the education of Dionysus. He is shown either as stately, inspired and tuneful, or as a drunken old man.

URANUS is a personification of heaven or the sky, the most ancient of the Greek gods and the first ruler of the universe.

ZEUS is the supreme god. He was the protector and ruler of humankind, the dispenser of good and evil, and the god of weather. He was identified with Jupiter by the Romans.

Greek Goddesses
ACHLYS is the Greek Mother—the first being to exist, according to myth. She gave birth to Chaos.

AMPHITRITE is a sea goddess, wife of Poseidon and mother of Triton.

APHRODITE is the goddess of beauty, fertility and sexual love, identified by the Romans with Venus. She is portrayed both as the daughter of Zeus and Dione, and as being born of the sea foam.

ARACHNE is a spider Goddess. Originally a mortal, she was a weaver who challenged Athene to compete with her. Athene was displeased by Arachne's subject matter, and in retribution turned her into a spider.

ARTEMIS, a hunter goddess, is often depicted with a bow and arrows and is associated with birth, fertility and abundance. She was identified with the Roman goddess Diana and with Selene.

ATHENE is identified with the Roman Minerva and often symbolized as an epitome of wisdom and strategy; she is also called Pallas. Statues show her as female and fully armed; the owl is regularly associated with her.

CYBELE is a goddess of caverns and of the primitive earth. Also known as a bee goddess, she ruled over wild beasts.

DEMETER is a corn and barley goddess, and also goddess of the earth in its productive state. She is the mother of Persephone. She is identified with Ceres and Cybele; her symbol is often an ear of corn.

HECATE, the goddess of dark places, is often associated with ghosts and sorcery, and is worshipped with offerings at crossroads. Identified as Queen of the Witches in the modern day, she is frequently identified with Artemis and Selene.

HERA was worshipped as the queen of heaven and a marriage goddess. The Romans identified her with Juno.

HESTIA is a goddess of hearth and fire, much like Brigid. She was believed to preside at all sacrificial altar fires, and prayers were offered to her before and after meals. In Rome, Hestia was worshipped as Vesta.

NEMESIS is a goddess usually portrayed as the agent of divine punishment for wrongdoing or presumption. She is often little more than the personification of retribution.

NIKE is the goddess of victory, who challenged her suitors to outrun her.

PERSEPHONE was called Proserpina by the Romans. From a magical perspective, her story symbolizes the return of fertility

to the earth. Hades, king of the underworld, wanted her as his wife, carrying her off and making her queen of the underworld. Demeter, her mother, unable to find her, began to pine, and famine began to spread around the world. Eventually it was agreed that she would spend six months on earth and six months in the underworld.

SELENE, the Goddess of the Moon, is identified with Artemis.

THEMIS is the daughter of Uranus (Heaven) and Gaia (Earth). She is the personification of order and justice, who convenes the assembly of the gods.

Roman Gods

CUPID is the god of love and was identified by the Romans with Eros. He is often pictured as a naked boy with wings, carrying a bow and arrow, with which he pierces his victims.

JANUS is an ancient Italian deity. He is guardian of doorways, gates and beginnings, and protector of the state in times of war. He is usually represented with two faces, so he looks both forward and backward.

JUPITER is the chief god of the Roman state, giver of victory, and is identified with Zeus. Also called Jove, he was originally a sky god associated with lightning and the thunderbolt. His wife was Juno.

MARS is the god of war and the most important god after Jupiter. He is identified with Ares by the Greeks, and was probably originally an agricultural god. The month of March is named after him.

MERCURY is the god of eloquence, skill, trading and thieving. He was a herald and messenger of the gods, who was identified with Hermes.

NEPTUNE is the god of water—originally fresh water, and later the sea. He is also the god of horse-racing, and is also identified with the Greek Poseidon.

PLUTO is the God of the Underworld and of transformation. He has responsibility for precious metals, and was sometimes known as the Rich One.

SATURN is an ancient god identified with the Greek Cronus, often regarded as a god of agriculture. His festival in December, Saturnalia, eventually became one of the elements in the traditional celebrations of Christmas.

SILVANUS is an Italian woodland deity identified with Pan. He is also worshipped in the Celtic religion.

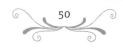

Roman Goddesses

ANGERONA is the goddess of secrecy and is portrayed with her mouth bound and sealed, and her finger raised to her mouth in a gesture of warning.

BONA DEA is an earth goddess of fertility who was worshipped by women only—no men were allowed present during her rites. The Romans would even cover up statues of the male gods when her rite was performed.

CERES, the corn goddess, is commonly identified by the Romans with Demeter.

DIANA is an early goddess identified with Artemis and associated with hunting, virginity and the Moon.

JUNO is an ancient mother goddess and became the most important goddess of the Roman state. She was the wife of Jupiter.

MINERVA is the goddess of handicrafts, commonly worshipped and associated with Athene. Because of this association, she came to be regarded as the goddess of war.

MUSES (Roman and Greek) are the goddesses who presided over the arts and sciences. Customarily nine in number (Calliope, Clio, Eurterpe, Terpsichore, Erato, Melpomene, Thalia, Polyhymnia and Urania), their functions and even their names differ widely among various sources.

VENUS, the supreme goddess of beauty, is identified with Aphrodite and was honored as the mother of the Roman people. In earlier times, she was a spirit of kitchen gardens.

VESTA, the goddess of the hearth and household, was considered important enough to have her own handmaidens, the Vestal Virgins.

Norse Gods and Goddesses

Deities in Scandinavia were originally of two kinds: Aesir and Vanir. The latter were largely nature deities rather than fertility gods and goddesses, and were incorporated into the former after warring with them. The Scandinavian creation myth is that the gods Odin, Vili and Ve, three brothers, were walking by the sea when they found two trees out of which they fashioned the parents of the human race, giving them spirit, life, wit, feeling, form and the five senses. They then retired to Asgard, where they dwelled in a great house called Gladsheim. Valhall in Gladsheim was Odin's place of the warriors, while Yggdrasil, the "World Tree"—a column sustaining everything—was a version of the Tree of Life. It is sometimes thought to be the sacred ash tree.

Norse Gods

There are many Scandinavian deities. Some of the most important ones to appeal to in spell-making are:

BALDER, whose name means bright, was the son of Odin and Frigg. The wisest of the gods, his judgments were final. He was killed by Loki, who gave him mistletoe, the only plant that had not agreed to protect him.

FREY is the God of Yule, traditionally born on the winter solstice, usually December 21st. He is a god of peace and plenty who brings fertility and prosperity. His effigy was paraded by the people on a wagon throughout the land, in the dead of winter.

LOKI is the personification of malicious mischief. Probably initially a fire god, he is supposed to bring the gods great hardship but also be able to relieve hardship. He is somewhat capricious and is not to be trusted. He is known as The Trickster.

NJORD rules the winds and quells both the sea and fire. He is appealed to when undertaking a journey and when hunting. He is worshipped by seafarers. Also the god of wealth, he is often coupled in toasts with his son, Frey.

ODIN (also Woden) is a magician and wise one. He learned the secrets of the runes by hanging himself from the ash tree Yggdrasil for nine nights. He was a shape-shifter and was known as Father of the Gods. Wednesday (Odin's Day) was named after him.

THOR is the Thunderer, who wields a divine hammer; he was the strongest of the Gods. His chariot racing across the sky is said to generate thunder, though other stories suggest this is done when he blows into his beard. He is also a fertility god. Thursday (Thor's Day) was named after him.

TYR is the god of battle, identified with Mars, after whom Tuesday is named.

Norse Goddesses

FREYA, the daughter of Njord, is the goddess of love, beauty and sexuality. She is said to choose the souls of those who have fallen in battle to take them to Valhalla (Odin's heaven). She is particularly skilled in magic.

FRIGG is Odin's wife and the foremost of the Asyngur (Goddesses). She is the patroness of the household and of married women. She was, and is, invoked by the childless. Also the mother of the Aesir, she gives her name to Friday. She was inadvertently instrumental in Balder's death—all things took oaths not to hurt him, except mistletoe, which was considered by Frigg to be too young.

IDUNN possessed the apples of immortality, which rejuvenated the gods when they grew old. Because Scandinavian gods were not immortal, they depended upon her and her good will for the continuation of life.

NORNS are the three virgin goddesses of destiny (Urd or Urder, Verdandi and Skuld). They sit by the Well of Fate at the base of the ash tree Yggdrasil and spin the Web of Fate.

OSTARA's symbols are the egg and the hare. While not strictly Nordic, she is a Germanic goddess of fertility who is celebrated at the time of the Spring Equinox. She was allegedly known by the Saxons as Eostre, the goddess of spring, from whom we derived the word Easter, although new research disputes this.

SKADI was the consort of Njord and is said to have preferred to live in the mountains rather than by the sea. She is the Goddess of death, independence and hunting.

South American Gods

BACABS (Mayan) are the gods of the four points of the compass, who hold up the sky. They are also lords of the seasons.

CHAC (Aztec and Mayan) is a rain and vegetation god. He is also the lord of thunder, lightning, wind and fertility, and is particularly revered by farmers.

CUPARA (Jivaro) and his wife are the parents of the Sun, and they created the Moon from mud to be his mate. The children of the Sun and Moon are the animals.

HUNAB KU (also known as Kinebahan) is the chief god of the Mayan pantheon, the Great God without Form, existing only in spirit.

HUEHUETEOTL (Aztec), a fire god, is also patron of warriors and kings. Associated with creation, he is often depicted as a crouched old man with a bowl of burning incense on his head.

HURAKAN (Mayan) is god of thunderstorms and the whirlwind. His name gave us the word "hurricane." At the behest of his friend Gucumatz, son of the Sun and the Moon, Hurakan created the world, the animals, men and fire.

IMAYMANA VIRACOCHA AND TOCAPO VIRACOCHA (Inca) are the sons of the creator god Viracocha. They gave names to all the trees, flowers, fruits and herbs, and supervised the people, telling them which could be eaten, which could cure, and which could kill.

INTI (Inca) is a Sun god. His image is a golden disk with a human face surrounded by bright rays. Every day Inti soars across the sky to the western horizon, plunges into the sea and swims under the earth back to the east. His sons, Viracocha, Manco Capac and Pachamac, are all creator gods.

ITZAMNA (Mayan) is a sky god and healer and son of Hunab Ku. God of drawing and letters, patron of learning and the sciences, Itzamna is said to be able to bring the dead back to life.

KINICH AHAU (also Ah Xoc Kin) (Mayan), the Sun god, is usually shown with jaguar features, wearing the symbol of Kin (the Mayan day). As Ah Xoc Kin, he was associated with music and poetry.

KUKULCAN (Mayan) is a serpent god and has similarities to Quetzalcoatl of the Aztecs.

NGURVILU (Araucanian, Chile) is god of lakes and seas.

QUETZALCOATL (Aztec) is an ancient deity and greatly revered; he is also believed to have been the creator god and is identified with the planet Venus. He is also identified with breath, wind, rain and sea breezes.

TEZCATLIPOCA (Aztec) is an all-powerful god who can see everything that happens in the world, as it is reflected in his mirror. He is associated with night, the jaguar, sorcery, natural forces, human strength, weakness, wealth, happiness and sorrow.

TUPAN (Tupinamba, Brazil) is god of thunder and lightning. When Tupan visits his mother, the passage of his boat causes storms. The Tupinamba respect, but do not worship, Tupan.

VIRACOCHA (Inca) means "sea foam." The creator and teacher of the world, Viracocha made people out of clay after the Great Flood. On each figure he painted the features, clothes and hairstyles of the many nations, and gave them languages, songs and the seeds they were to plant. Bringing them to life, Viracocha ordered them to travel underground and emerge at different places on the earth. Then Viracocha made the Sun, Moon and stars, and assigned them their places in the sky.

South American Goddesses

EVAKI (Bakairi) is goddess of night. She is said to place the Sun in a pot every night and move it back to its starting point in the east every day.

IX CHEL (Maya) is consort of Itzamna and goddess of the Moon, weaving and medicine. Except for Hunab Ku, all the other gods are the progeny of Ix Chel and Itzamna.

MAMA QUILLA (Inca) is goddess of the Moon and protector of married women. Her image is a silver disc with a human face.

XOCHIQUETZAL (Aztec), originally a Moon goddess of the earth, flowers, plants, games and dance, is principally a goddess of love. Also beloved of artisans and pregnant women, she is the most charming of the Aztec pantheon. She is responsible for butterflies—symbolic of love, death and rebirth, transformation, hope, freedom, and spiritual awakening— as well as birds.

Oceanic Gods and Goddesses

There are many gods and goddesses indigenous to the Oceanic region, and the few mentioned here show the similarities among various creation myths.

BUNJIL (Australia) is a sky god. He made men out of clay while his brother, Bat, made women out of water. To mankind, Bunjil gave tools, weapons and religious ceremony.

DARAMULUN (Australia) is a sky god, a hero. There are many tales of his adventures. Daramulun is usually portrayed with a mouth full of quartz and a huge phallus, carrying a stone axe.

DREAM TIME (Australia) is the period of creation when the gods brought the world and all living creatures into being.

GIDJA (Australia) is a Moon god. In the Dream Time, Gidja created women by castrating Yalungur, for which he was punished by Kallin Kallin. Gidja floated out to sea and ended up in the sky, where he became the Moon.

GREAT RAINBOW SNAKE (Australia) is also known by many other names. The great giver of life, he lives in a deep pool. He stretches across the sky and shines with water drops, quartz and mother of pearl, whose iridescence holds his life force. In the Dream Time, the Great Rainbow Snake created all waterways—which must not be contaminated with blood—and all living creatures.

IO (New Zealand) is the Supreme Being of the Maori, master of all the other gods, known only to the priesthood.

KALLIN KALLIN (Australia) punished Gidja for castrating his brother Yalungur, the Eaglehawk. Kallin Kallin then took Yalungur as his wife, and established the custom among indigenous Australians of taking wives from different communities.

MAUI (Polynesia) is a trickster and a hero god. He lived when the world was still being created, and fought on the side of humankind. Maui raised the sky and snared the sun. His death at the hands of Hina brought death into the world.

PELE (Polynesia) is goddess of volcanic fire and sorcery. She lives on Mount Kilauea in Hawaii. Altars to her are built beside lava streams; only her descendants worship her.

QAT (Polynesia) is a creator god. Qat was born when his mother, a stone, exploded. He made the first three pairs of men and women by carving them from wood and playing drums to make them dance. He stopped night from going on forever by cutting it with a red stone, which is the dawn. Qat sailed away in a canoe filled with all manner of wonderful things, leaving behind the legend that he would one day return.

TAWHAKI (Polynesia) is the god of thunder and lightning. He is said to be noble and handsome.

TU (Polynesia) is a god of war, and one of the most widely worshipped gods of Polynesia.

WONDJINA (Australia) are the primordial beings of the Dream Time, who created the world. They give both rain and children, and the paintings depicting them are refreshed every year so that they will continue to bring rain at the end of the dry season.

YALUNGUR (Australia) defeated the terrible ogress Kunapipi, was castrated by Gunja, and thus became the first woman.

THE ARCHANGELS

The four archangels can be found in a variety of protective incantations and invocations. Their purpose is to guard the four quarters or cardinal points. They are an almost universal symbol that can turn up in many different aspects, from nursery rhymes to the guardians of the dead.

For our purposes, they might be thought of as extra help in living our lives successfully. Think of yourself making a connection to Michael so you can love more fully; to Gabriel for strength, to fill you with power for the next day; to Uriel for suffusing you with the light of the mind or understanding; and to Raphael for healing your ills. When you are having a hard time, you can send a brief prayer or request to whichever one is most appropriate.

Generally, there are considered to be seven archangels, and it will depend on your own teachings as to which school of thought you follow in naming them. Because the teachings were initially by word of mouth, there are different lists of archangels deputed to help the world on its way. The four archangels considered here are the ones that appear consistently in most lists, and are therefore the best known universally. They are the ones most often called upon in magical workings. The only problem is that sometimes Michael and Uriel appear to swap places in some traditions, which can be confusing. If the attributions given here do not feel right, try the ritual the other way around, and change the words accordingly. Make sure you still call upon all four archangels, however.

MICHAEL means "who is as God" in Hebrew. The Roman Catholic Church regards Michael in much the same light as does the Church of England, with his festival, Michaelmas, being held on September 29th. He is known in mythology as the one who attempted to bring Lucifer back to God. In Ezekiel's vision of the cherubim, or the four sacred animals, he is the angel with the face of the lion. Michael is often visualized as a masculine archangel dressed in robes or armor of red and green. He stands in the attitude of a warrior amid flames. Bearing either a sword or a spear, Michael is the guardian against evil and the protector of humanity. He is stationed in the south.

RAPHAEL is one of four archangels stationed around the throne of God; his task is to heal the earth. Initially he was pictured with the face of a dragon, but this was changed in later imagery to the face of a man. He is often visualized as a tall, fair figure standing on the clouds in robes of yellow and violet, sometimes holding the Caduceus of Hermes as a symbol of his healing powers. He is God's builder or composer, and has the task of building or rebuilding the earth, which the fallen angels have defiled. Raphael's name in Hebrew means "Healer of God" or "God Has Healed." Raphael Ruachel ("Raphael of Air") is stationed in the east.

In Hebrew, **GABRIEL** means "Strong One of God." He is one of the four archangels who stand in the presence of God, and was sent to announce to Mary the birth of Jesus. In Ezekiel's vision of the four sacred animals, he has the face of the eagle. Gabriel is often visualized as a feminine archangel holding a cup, standing on the waters of the sea and wearing robes of blue and orange. Gabriel is also at one with the higher ego or inner divinity. Gabriel Maimel ("Gabriel of Water") is stationed in the west.

URIEL (or Auriel's) name in Hebrew means "Light of God." Specifically, he is the angel or divinity of light—not simply of physical light, but of spiritual illumination. Also referred to as "The Angel of Repentance," he is the angel of terror, prophecy and mystery. He was sometimes ranked as an archangel with Michael, Gabriel, and Raphael, and is believed to hold the keys to the gates of Hell.

He is also often identified as the angel who drove Adam and Eve from the Garden of Eden, and was thought to be the messenger sent to warn Noah of the floods. As "Uriel Aretziel" ("Uriel of Earth") he is stationed in the north. He is often seen rising from the vegetation of the earth holding stems of ripened wheat, wearing robes of citrine, russet, olive and black.

ARCHANGELS AND THE ELEMENTALS

Each archangel of the Elements has as his servant one of the kings of the Elemental kingdoms. By tradition, each of the Elements ties in with certain nature spirits, of which the dryads are only one kind. They are:

Air
Raphael has as his servant Paralda, King of the Sylphs, who appears to clairvoyant vision as a form made of blue mist that's always moving and changing shape.

Fire
Michael is accompanied by Djinn, King of the Salamanders, who appears as a Fire giant composed of living flame surrounded by fiery sparks that crackle and glow.

Water
Gabriel's servant is Nixa, King of the Undines, seen as an ever-changing shape, fluid with a greenish blue aura splashed with silver and gray.

Earth

Uriel is served by Ghob, King of the Gnomes, traditionally seen as a squat, heavy and dense gnome or goblin.

You do not have to call on these Elementals in your rituals, but you should be aware of their energies in that they are the servants of the archangels, and not yours.

PETITIONING THE ARCHANGELS

This spell uses the higher aspects of the guardians of the directions and petitions the four archangels according to their qualities—Michael for love, Gabriel for strength, Raphael for healing and Uriel for clarity. Uriel, the "light of God," is represented by the candles. When you perceive a lack of something in your life, petitioning the archangels helps fulfill it.

You will need

- Four white candles
- Plate on which you have scattered sugar

Method

Stand the candles on the plate and scatter the sugar all around them. Light the candles. Put the plate and candles in the highest place you can safely reach at home. This signifies the status we give the archangels. You may now ask for three wishes from them. Keep in mind that you may only petition the archangels if it is important.

If you like, address each of the archangels by name, or use the same invocation below.

This protects you from inadvertently making silly mistakes. The words are:

Before me Raphael
Behind me Gabriel
On my right hand Michael
On my left hand Uriel
God be thanked.

Let the candles burn out.

Share this spell with others on the third day (after you requested the wishes) and help pass on the benefit of your gain. You should use this spell wisely and not make ridiculous requests with it. If what you wish does not happen, accept that it is not right for you to make the wish, and do not repeat the request.

SACRED SPACE

If you are going to be carrying out a fair number of rituals or spells, you will need a sacred space or altar, and altar furnishings. If it is indoors, your altar and/or sacred space should be in a quiet place in your home, where it will not be disturbed and where candles can be burned safely.

The space needs to be dedicated to the purpose of magical working. You can do this by first brushing the area clean with an ordinary brush, concentrating your thoughts on cleansing the space as you work. Mentally cleanse the space three times, imagining doing it once for the physical world, once for the emotional space, and once spiritually.

If you wish, you may sprinkle the whole area with water and salt (which represents the earth). You might also burn incense to clear the atmosphere. Think of the space as somewhere you would entertain an honored guest in your home. You will later use your besom to keep the sacred space clear.

If you travel a lot, or are short on space, you may dedicate a tray or special piece of wood or china for ceremonial working. This, along with your candles and incense, can be kept together in a small box. Otherwise, you could dedicate a table especially for the purpose. Ideally, you should not need to pack up each time.

You will also need a "fine cloth"—the best you can afford—to cover the surface. Place the cloth on your surface and spend some quiet time just thinking about its purpose. You may have different cloths for different purposes, or just one cloth, which is "dressed" with the appropriate color for each ritual.

Setting up your altar

To turn your table into a proper altar, you will need the following objects:

1. Two candles with candle holders—you might think of one representing the female principle and one the male. In addition, you may also choose candles of a color suitable for the ritual or spell you are working.

2. An incense holder, and appropriate incense.

3. A representation of the deity or deities you prefer to work with; it could be anything from a statue to bowls, or stones.

4. A vase for flowers or fresh herbs. As mentioned in the Tools section on pages 14-16, there are other objects that you might need for your ceremonial working. Briefly, these are an athame, a boline, a burin, a

small bowl or cauldron, a bowl of water, a bowl of salt or sand, and a consecrated cloth, on which to place dedicated objects.

Some people also use bells to summon the powers of the Elements, while others have additional candles with the colors representing themselves or the work they wish to do. You can add other items to your altar, such as amulets and talismans.

Dedicating your altar

Now that you have turned your space into an altar, dedicate it in such a way that it will support your workings. One good way is to dedicate it to the principle of the Greater Good—that none may be harmed by anything you do. (Remember that, traditionally, any harm you instigate deliberately will return to you threefold, particularly when it comes from such a sacred space.)

Put passion and energy into the dedication, and remember to include a prayer for protection of your sacred space. Some people will need to cast a circle each time they do a working, while others will feel that just by setting the altar up in the way suggested, the space is consecrated.

Dedicate your tools and altar furnishings to the purpose at hand. You are empowering them and making them usable only in ritual and magical work. If you try to use them for any other purpose, you will negate that magical power.

Consecrating altar objects

If you are not using new objects as the basic furnishings (such as candle holders) on your altar, cleanse them before you dedicate them to your purpose. Soak them overnight in salt water to remove anyone else's vibrations, then place them in sunshine (or moonshine) for at least twelve hours to charge them with appropriate energy.

When you are ready, hold each object and allow your energy to flow into it, followed by the energy of your idea of Ultimate Power. Ask this Power to bless the object and any working you do with it, and perceive yourself as a medium or channel for the energy.

Finally, if you wish, create and cast your circle (see below) so that it includes yourself and your altar. The magic circle defines the ritual area, holds in personal power and shuts out distractions and negative energies.

Casting a circle

Purify yourself first by meditating or taking a ritual bath. One way is to try to keep the water flowing, possibly by leaving the bath plug half in, or by having a shower. This reinforces the idea of washing away impurities so you are not sitting in your own psychic garbage. Ideally, your towel—if you choose to use one—should be clean and used only for the purpose of your ritual bath.

Wear something special if you can, something you only wear for magical work. This sets it apart from your everyday life.

Decide on the extent of your circle, which should be formed in front of your altar. Purify the space by sprinkling the area with water followed by salt—both of these should have been blessed or consecrated in some way with simple words.

Sit quietly for as long as you can inside the area that will become your circle. Imagine a circle of white, blue or purple light surrounding you. If you are in a hurry and cannot purify and cleanse fully, reinforce the circle of light by visualizing it suffused with the appropriate color for your working.

Circle the light around, above and below you in a clockwise direction, like the representation of an atom. Feel it as a sphere or as a cone of power. Sense the power. Remember that you can create a "doorway" through which your magical energy may exit. You should always feel warm and peaceful inside your circle. As time goes on, you will be able to differentiate between the various energies at play here.

Use a personal chant or words, according to your own belief system, to consecrate your circle and banish evil and negative energy, forbidding anything harmful to enter your space. Remember, you are always safe in your circle if you command it to be so.

If you wish, invite the gods and goddesses to attend your circle and magical working. Relax and be happy. You can use objects on the ground to show the boundaries of the circle, such as candles, cord, stones or flowers. The circle is formed from personal power. This may be felt and visualized as streaming from the body to form a bubble made of mist, or a circle of light. You can use the athame or your hands to direct this power.

The cardinal points of the compass may be denoted with lit candles, often white or purple. Alternatively, place a green candle at the north point of the circle, a yellow candle at the east, a red candle at the south and a blue candle at the west. The altar stands in the center of the circle, facing north in the direction of power.

An Alternative Method of Circle Casting

This method probably owes more to the practices of Wicca than any other way, though you do not have to be Wiccan to use it.

You will need
- Besom
- Ritual tools (athame, etc.)
- Candle to represent your working
- Altar candles to represent the Goddess and God
- A heatproof dish, if you are using incense
- Compass (to work out directions)
- Candle snuffer

Method

Cleanse the sacred space symbolically with the besom. Place the altar in the center of the circle facing north. Set up the altar as described on pages 61-62. Start with the candle representing the Goddess on the left, and the God on the right. In the middle, follow with the candle that represents your magical working.

Move toward the northern edge of the area you are enclosing. Light the incense.

Hold your left hand out, palm down, at waist level. Point your fingers toward the edge of the circle you are creating. (You can, of course, use your athame if you have consecrated it.)

See and feel the energy flowing out from your fingertips (or the athame), and slowly walk the circle, clockwise. Think of the energy your body is generating.

Continue to move clockwise, gradually increasing your pace as you do so.

Move faster until you feel the energy flowing inside you. The energy will move with you as you release it.

Sense your personal power creating a sphere of energy around the altar. When this is firmly established, call on the Elements that rule the four directions.

Your circle is now consecrated and ready for you to use for whatever magical purpose you need. You will require the candle snuffer to safely close your circle after you have finished your magical working.

Ending your magical working

When you have finished your ritual or working, remind yourself that you are as pure a channel for the energies that you have called upon as possible. These energies *must* be returned from whence they came, so visualize them passing through you and being returned. At the same time, remember that you are blessed by these energies and by the fact that you have used them with good intent.

Closing a Circle

Thank the Elements' rulers, if you have called upon them, for attending the ritual. If you used ritual tools, holding your athame, stand at the north. Pierce the circle's wall with the blade at waist level. If you wish, simply use your index finger instead.

Move clockwise around the circle. Visualize its power being sucked back into the knife or your finger. Sense the sphere of energy withdrawing and dissipating.

Let the outside world slowly make itself felt in your consciousness. As you come back to the north again, the energy of the circle should have disappeared. If it has not, simply repeat the actions. If you have laid items to mark out the circle, remove them. If you have used salt and water, you may save the excess salt for future uses, but pour the water onto the bare earth. Bury any ashes.

Put out the candles. Put away your tools respectfully if you are not able to leave your altar in place.

PART II
THE SPELLS

WHAT IS A SPELL?

There are three important aspects to reciting a spell. The first is that words spoken with intensity and passion have a power all their own. The next is that the speaker also has a power and an energy that, with practice, they may learn to use effectively. The third component, the forces and powers belonging to that which is "beyond the human being" also has tremendous power, and is used for a specific purpose. The combination of all of these aspects gives a very powerful spell indeed.

There are several kinds of spell, each of which requires a different approach.

LOVE SPELLS

Love spells should be unconditional, unselfish and free of self-interest. However, most of the time they obviously cannot be so, unless they are performed by a third party.

To try and influence someone else goes against the ethics of many practitioners and magicians. Anyone who wishes to experiment with love spells needs to be aware that such spells come under the category of bidding spells, and therefore must be used carefully.

BIDDING SPELLS

These are spells where the spell-maker commands a particular thing to happen, but without the cooperation of those involved. Trying to make someone do something that goes against their natural inclination can misfire, causing the originator of the spell a good deal of difficulty.

Preface such spells with words to signify that the outcome will only be in accord with the greater good—that is, that in the overall scheme of things no one will be harmed. This ensures that the intent behind the spell is pure, and that there is no malice on the part of the practitioner. An able and responsible practitioner must choose their words carefully, even when they are not casting a spell.

BLESSINGS

These hold no danger for the practitioner but are sometimes more difficult to appreciate since they tend to be more general than other types of magical work. They may be thought of in terms of a positive energy from beyond the practitioner, being channeled toward a specific purpose.

Saying grace before a meal is a form of blessing preceded by an offer of praise and a prayer of gratitude, an acknowledgment of a gift. The food is enhanced by the act and the blessing is given by drawing on the power vested in the expert.

HEALING SPELLS AND CHARMS

For this type of spell, it is wise to look beyond symptoms and ask for healing on all levels—physical, mental and spiritual—because the practitioner may not be capable of diagnosing a condition. The energies and vibrations are enhanced by invocations, incantations and blessings wherever appropriate.

INVOCATIONS

These call on what is believed to be the ultimate source of power, which differs from spell to spell. They call up that power and ask for permission to use this influence for a stated purpose. Meddling with this power and calling up negative forces is foolish.

INCANTATIONS

This type of spell prepares the magical worker and his helpers for further work by heightening their awareness. It does not set out to call up the powers, but appeals to gods, goddesses, powers of nature and so on for help.

Chanting, prayer and hymns are in many ways incantations, particularly when the intent is stated with some passion. An incantation is often very beautiful and rhythmic. Music has always been an efficient way of heightening awareness and altering states of consciousness.

THE ELEMENTS

As previously mentioned on pages 16-19, in most systems of magical working you will find the four (or sometimes five) Elements—Earth, Air, Fire and Water—often in conjunction with their directions or, as they are known in magic, quarters of the universe or cardinal points. They are powerful sources of energy and can give a tremendous boost to spell-making. Each Element also comes under the protection of one of the Archangels (see pages 58-60).

The fifth Element is that of spirit, the "binding principle" behind everything. Sometimes known as "the ether," it is intangible, but it makes everything happen. You are its representative and its channel, so in using the other Elements in magical working you must act wisely and well.

FRIENDSHIP, LOVE, AND RELATIONSHIPS

TO ATTRACT A NEW FRIEND

This spell draws to you a friend rather than a lover. Perform it during a waxing Moon.

You will need
• Three brown candles
• Sheet of paper
• Pen

Method
Light the candles. On the sheet of paper, write down the attributes you would like your friend to have. Say each one out loud. Fold the paper in half twice. Light the edge of the folded paper from one of the candles and repeat the words below:

With heart and mind I do now speak
Bring to me the one I seek
Let this paper be the guide
And bring this friend to my side.
Pain and loneliness be no more
Draw a companion to my door.
With pleasures many and sorrows few
Let us build a friendship new.

Let not this simple spell coerce
Or make my situation worse.
As I will, it shall be.

Let the paper burn out, then snuff out the candles. Use these candles only for the same type of spell.

In the next few weeks, you should meet someone with some or all of the qualities you seek. Remember that you have called this person to you, so explore the relationship properly. Never be judgmental about qualities in your new friend that are not ones you requested.

TO BRING ROMANTIC LOVE TO YOU

This spell uses herbs, crystals, candle and color. Rosemary traditionally signifies long memory, the rose quartz crystal signifies love, and the colors signify love and passion. It is designed to concentrate the mind and attract love to you, as opposed to a specific lover.

You will need

- Small box
- Red marker/pen
- Rose or vanilla incense
- A sprig of rosemary (for remembrance)
- A piece of rose quartz crystal
- Pink or red votive candle

Method

Sit in your most powerful place—inside, outside, near your favorite tree or by running water. Write in red on the box:

> Love is mine.

Light the incense—this clears the atmosphere and puts you in the right mood. Put the rosemary and rose quartz in the box.

Put anything else that represents love to you in the box (poems, drawings of hearts, or whatever—be creative).

Remember, this spell is to attract love to you, not a specific lover. So don't use a representation of a particular person.

Be in a positive state of mind.

Imagine yourself happy and in love.

Light the candle and say:

> I am love
> love I will find
> true love preferably
> will soon be mine

> Love is me
> Love I seek
> my true love
> I will soon meet.

Now sit for a little while and concentrate again on being happy.

Pinch or snuff out the candle and add it to the box. Let the incense burn out.

Seal the box shut and don't open it until you have found your true love.

When you have found your lover, take the rose quartz out of the box and keep it as a reminder. Bury the entire box in the earth.

Because in this spell you reproduce a positive state of mind and you are imagining what it is like to be in love, you set up a current of energy that attracts the same feeling. In sealing the box you are "capturing" the vibration of love, and all things then become possible.

TO OBTAIN LOVE FROM A SPECIFIC PERSON

This spell uses fire as its vehicle, in a cauldron. You use an incantation, and can also use magical ink and parchment if you wish. The spell is best done at night, and using the power of the number three is not just for lust but also for love.

You will need
- Your cauldron or a fireproof container
- A piece of paper
- Pen and red ink
- Fragrant wood or herbs to burn (you could use apple, birch or cedar)

Method
Light a small fire in your cauldron or a suitable container.

Cut out a piece of paper that is 3 x 3 inches (10 cm x 10 cm).

With the pen and red ink, draw a heart on the paper, and color it. Write the name of the person you desire on the heart three times.

If you like, do this from the edge to the middle in a spiral, to signify how deep your love goes.

While doing this, think of their heart burning with desire for you, just like the flames of the fire.

Kiss the names on the heart three times. Place the paper in the fire while saying these words three times:

Soon my love will come to me
This I know that it must be
Fire come from this wood
Bring love and caring that it would
Make our hearts glow and shine,
Bringing love that shall be mine!

Sit quietly as the paper burns, visualizing your lover coming to you.

After you are finished concentrating for a few minutes, extinguish the fire.

Say quietly three times:

So, let it be

Do not get impatient if nothing happens for a while. Simply have faith that you will be given an opportunity to have a relationship with this person. How you handle the relationship thereafter is entirely up to you.

TO GAIN CONFIDENCE IN SOCIAL SITUATIONS

Charm bags are an efficient way of carrying reminders that can add zest to life. This one is used to help overcome shyness, perhaps when you are meeting new people or doing something you have never done before. This spell is also useful if you suffer from a lack of confidence in a general sense. It is best done during the waxing Moon.

You will need
- A small drawstring bag about 1-2 inches (2.5-5 cm) deep; you could use a color such as yellow to enhance communication

- Ground nutmeg
- Pine needles
- Dried lavender
- Piece of mandrake root

Method

Put a pinch or two of the nutmeg, pine needles, dried lavender and mandrake root in the bag and close it.

Consecrate and charge the bag during the waxing phase of the Moon so you can use positive energy. Wear the bag around your neck or keep it in your pocket. You should feel a surge of energy whenever you are in a social situation you find difficult to handle. When you feel you no longer need the support your bag gives you, scatter the herbs to the four winds or burn them in your cauldron.

It is the consecrating of the bag that turns it into a tool for use in everyday situations, so choose your words carefully to express your particular need. Try to approach one new person every day, or go into one new situation, until you lose your fear.

HERBAL HEARTSEASE

Broken relationships are extremely painful, and the hurt often needs to be dealt with quickly. This spell, using three techniques, helps keep things under control until you can look forward in a positive fashion.

Cleansing bath

You will need

- Handful of heartsease, or/and jasmine, roses, hibiscus and honeysuckle flowers
- Essential oils in any of these perfumes
- Rose quartz

Method

Add the herbs to the bathtub along with the essential oils. Then add the rose quartz. Soak in the bath for at least ten minutes, allowing the hurt to be dissolved. Remove the rose quartz. Take the plug halfway out, so the water begins to drain away. As it does so, replace it with fresh water to signify new energy coming into your life. Carry the rose quartz with you or keep it under your pillow.

Healing sachet

You will need

- Two 4-inch squares of red or white fabric
- Needle with pink thread
- Herbs, as above
- Small piece of rose or clear quartz
- Small quantity of dried beans

Method

Make a sachet by sewing together three sides of the fabric with the pink thread.

Fill the sachet with the herbs, quartz and beans, then sew up the fourth side.

As you sew, know that the pain will pass.

Hang the sachet in a prominent position so you can feel its healing vibration.

Healing face wash

You will need
- Herbs, as above
- Boiling water
- Heatproof bowl (clear glass if possible)
- Glass bottle

Method

Place the herbs in the bowl and pour boiling water over them; allow the liquid to cool.

If you wish, allow it to stand overnight in moonlight to absorb its power.

Pour the liquid into a clean bottle and, using a cotton ball, wash your face with it. As you do so, remind yourself that you are lovable and will heal from this hurt.

These techniques are both gentle in their action and supportive on an emotional level. Working in three ways, they allow body, mind and spirit to be relaxed and at peace.

TO CREATE OPPORTUNITIES FOR LOVE

This is not a spell to draw a person to you, but to "open the way"—to alert the other person to the possibility of a relationship with you. The spell should be performed on a Friday. The use of your mother's ring is symbolic of continuity.

You will need
- A wine glass
- A ring (traditionally, your mother's wedding ring would be used)
- Red silk ribbon 30 inches (80cm) long

Method

Put a wine glass right side up on a table.

Make a pendulum by suspending the ring from the ribbon.

Hold the pendulum steady by resting your elbow on the table, with the ribbon between your thumb and forefinger. Let the ring hang in the mouth of the wine glass.

Clearly say your name followed by that of the other person. Say their name three times in total. Then, thinking of them, spell their name out loud. Allow the ring to swing and gently tap against the wine glass, once for each letter of their name. Tie the ribbon around your neck, allowing

the ring to hang down, close to your heart.

Wear it for three weeks, and repeat the spell every Friday for three weeks.

By the end of the third week, the person you have in your sights will show an interest, unless it is not meant to be.

Let's assume there is someone in whom you are interested, but the interest does not seem mutual. This spell ensures there are no hindrances, but there has to be at least some feeling for it to stand a chance of working.

TO FORGET ABOUT AN EX-LOVER

This spell should be done at the waning Moon or New Moon. It is not to get rid of a former partner, but to exorcise your bad feelings about them; finish the spell by sending them loving thoughts. Woody nightshade is poisonous, so you may not want to use it; if that is the case, use a bulb of garlic.

You will need
- Photograph of your ex-partner
- Suitable container for burning the photograph (one in which the ashes can be saved)
- Root of bittersweet (woody nightshade, which is poisonous) or a bulb of garlic
- Red cloth or bag

Method
Place the picture of your ex-partner in the container. Set it alight.

Gather up all your hurt and pain as the picture burns down. Feel them flowing away from you as you say these words or similar:

*Leave my heart and leave me free
Leave my life, no pain for me.
As this picture burns to dust,
Help me now, move on I must.*

Repeat the words until only ashes remain. Taking the herb root or garlic, hold it to your solar plexus (just above your belly button).

Allow the bad feelings to flow into the root or garlic. Touch the root or garlic to your forehead, indicating that you have converted the bad feelings to good.

Wrap everything, including the container of ashes, in your red bag or cloth.

As soon as possible, bury it as far away from your home as you can.

If you have had a relationship that was argumentative and turned nasty, it is often better to end it and move on. This must always be your choice, but if you wish to try again you may like to try the To Stop an Argument spell opposite.

TO HAVE YOUR LOVE RETURNED

This spell is candle magic and also representational. It is a little more complicated than most because it requires an understanding of symbolism. It is best done on a Friday. The objects you use need not be the real thing—they can be miniaturizations, such as cake decorations.

You will need
- Pink candle
- Blue candle
- Gold candle (to represent the relationship)
- Horseshoe (to represent luck in love)
- Key (to represent the key to your heart)
- Two roses
- An article of your love interest's clothing (failing that, a square of pink material)

Method
Light the pink and blue candles (pink first if you identify as a woman, blue if you identify as a man, or whichever your preference is if you're non-binary), followed by the gold.

Place the horseshoe and key on either side of the candles, with the roses between them.

When the candles have burned down, wrap the flowers, the key and the horseshoe in the clothing.

Place the items in a bedroom drawer and leave them alone for fourteen days. If after this time the flowers are still fresh, it is a good sign. You should bury them or, if you prefer, put them (along with the horseshoe and key) in potpourri.

You might use this spell when you think a relationship with someone would be worthwhile. If you can't find an article of the other person's clothing, a handkerchief or some other small article will do. If that is not possible, use a square of pink material.

TO GET RID OF AN UNWANTED ADMIRER

Occasionally people are pursued by someone whose attention is a nuisance. Rather than reacting in anger, it is often easier to open the way for the person to leave. This spell, done on a Waning Moon, often does the trick.

You will need
• Vervain leaves
• A fierce fire

Method
Light a fire. Pick up the vervain and, as you do so, call out the name of the offending person.

Fling the leaves on the fire and say:

*Withdraw from me now I need
you not.*

There is a requirement to declaim passionately, and to use some force, in any spell that is designed to drive someone from you. Therefore, be sure you do not want this person in your life in any way.

Ensure that the fire is safely extinguished. Repeat the action three nights in a row.

This spell should be performed outdoors, but it can be performed indoors if you have a suitable fireplace, and provided you are careful. Traditionally, one is supposed to gather the vervain leaves, but for most people that's a tall order. Make sure you have at least a couple of handfuls of the dried herb.

TO STOP AN ARGUMENT

This is a spell to stop an argument between you and another person. You are using color and representational magic here. So you don't let your feelings intrude, you might take a ritual bath first. The plate is used for two reasons in this spell: first, being glass, it reflects back to the person; and second, through its color it raises the whole question to its highest vibration.

You will need
• Glass plate (deep purple if possible, but

if not, clear will work just as well)
• Picture of the person with whom you have argued

Method

Place the picture face down on the plate for no more than 15 minutes. You do not want to over-influence the recipient, so spend a few moments remembering the good times you have had.

For this reason, if using an ordinary photograph, you should also be aware of where the negative to the picture is so that you are only using positive energy.

The person should communicate in some way within 24 hours, so you can resolve your difficulties. If they don't, repeat the procedure for no more than 15 minutes.

If after a third time you still haven't heard from them, try to give them a call or visit them, because their feelings should have changed somewhat.

You will then know that you have done all you can to be on good terms with them.

It is often difficult to get back onto a normal footing after an argument, so be prepared to apologize for any part you have played. Remember, you are only dealing with that particular argument, not deeper issues in the friendship.

A LOVER'S TOKEN

This bottle is a nice one to give your lover to intensify the link between you. The herbs are all well known for their association with love, and the link between the bottles should help you communicate.

You will need

For each token:
• A glass bottle with a cork
• A handful of dried rose petals (preferably from flowers given to you by your lover)
• Dried or fresh rosemary (for love and strength)
• Dried or fresh lavender
• Rose oil or water
• Wax (pink or red is good for love)
• Pink ribbon

Method

Crush the rose petals and place them in the bottle. Put in the rosemary and/or lavender, then add the oil or rose water almost to the top, leaving some room for air to circulate.

Cork the bottle and drip wax over the cork to seal it. Make another token bottle in the same way.

Put the ribbon on a flat surface. Place the bottles at either end of the ribbon.

Gradually move the bottles toward one another along the ribbon to signify you meeting with your lover.

When they meet, tie the ribbon around your partner's bottle and give it to them.

Place yours on a shelf, dresser or anywhere it will not be disturbed.

These bottles are tangible evidence of the link between you and your lover. You may use them to remind you of the good times or soothe you in the bad. The ribbon signifies the link between you, so when you think of it you will have immediately connected.

TO REKINDLE YOUR LOVER'S INTEREST

This technique is worth trying when your lover is not paying you enough attention. You are using the laurel leaves to back up the energy you are putting into making the relationship work. This spell uses herbal and elemental magic.

You will need
• A large quantity of laurel leaves
• A fire

Method
Sit in front of the embers of a fire and gaze into them, concentrating on your lover.

Keep your gaze fixed into the fire.

With your left hand, throw some laurel leaves onto the embers.

As they burn, say:

Laurel leaves burn into the fire.
Bring to me my heart's desire.

Wait until the flames die down, then do it again.

Repeat the actions once more.

It is said that within 24 hours your lover will come back to you.

Again, this is a spell that must allow the person you are targeting choices. To keep your partner by your side if they are unhappy would not be right. This spell allows you to give careful consideration as to what fidelity and security you require in a relationship.

RESOLVING A LOVE TRIANGLE

Sometimes it is possible to get caught up in a situation where three people are in a love triangle. It would be wrong to influence anyone one way or another, so here is a way of resolving the situation that should not harm anyone. It is best done at the time of the Full Moon.

You will need
- Three lengths of string, each about 1 yard (1 meter) long
- An open space where you will not be disturbed

Method
Form a triangle on the ground with the three pieces of string so that the ends are just touching.

Step into the middle of the triangle.

Appeal to the Triple Goddess in her guise of Maid, Mother and Crone. Use words such as:

Triple Goddess hear my plea
I ask you now to set us free
It's not a problem I can alter
So help me now lest I falter.

These words put you in touch with your inner self, which means that you decide what is right for you.

Wait for a few moments to allow the energy to build up, then raise your arms in a V shape (the Goddess position) and say:
So let it be.

Allow yourself time to consider the problem from all perspectives before making a decision as to how you should act. Each time you consider the position, remember to repeat the first two lines of the verse above.

It usually takes a little time for a situation like this to reach a resolution, but this spell allows you to feel supported and cared for. Gradually you will come to understand the action you must take, and you can accept that it is ultimately the best outcome for everyone.

TO ASK FOR A COMMITMENT

You may only ask the Universe to get your lover to commit to you if it is in everyone's best interest and reflects the true desire of their heart. This is best done on a waxing Moon.

You will need
- Magically charged paper and pen
- An ivy leaf

Method
Trace the outline of the ivy leaf on your charged piece of paper. Inside the outline, write out the specific commitment you want from your lover. It may be that you just want them to commit to seeing you twice a week; or it may be a more traditional commitment such as a handfasting. Then put your initials and those of your lover at the end of the outline. Cut around the outline and take it to running water—a stream, river or ocean. Cast the paper leaf into the water, saying:

Ivy true, Ivy faithful,
Pledge my love to me.

Then watch the paper leaf be carried away. Your lover should awpproach you regarding more commitment sooner rather than later.

The ivy plant is connected to fidelity since it thrives when it clings. However, take care not to be too clingy in relationships; even traditional handfastings only lasted a year and a day.

HEALTH, HEALING, AND WELLBEING

The subtle energies that come together to give each person their unique makeup are very precious, and can be conserved and enhanced. We as spell-workers have a responsibility to make ourselves as healthy and whole as possible, and in so doing can also help others overcome difficulties.

TO FORM A HEALTHY HABIT

Sometimes we want to behave in a way that we know is better for our health and wellbeing—be that exercising, eating well or remembering to relax or meditate regularly. This spell uses nuts (or any other small snack) to allow you to visualize how far you've come in building a new healthy habit. Start this spell on a New Moon, and keep in mind that you must commit to it—and your new habit—for a full lunar month.

You will need
- 28 pine nuts (or other small snack, such as chocolate chips)
- A dinner candle
- Burin

Method
Put the bowl of nuts on your altar. Then use your burin to mark 28 equal sections on your dinner candle. Light the candle and say these words:

With body and mind
I seek to find
A balance that is rightfully mine
A habit now I try to form
A break for good from my usual norm
Lady true, bring me health
Lady true, give me strength
So mote it be!

Now, each day of the next 28 days, light the candle at the start of the day and meditate on what it is you want to achieve with your healthy new habit. Let the candle burn down to that day's segment. At the end of the day, when you have practiced your healthy habit, consume one pine nut. By the end of the lunar month, all the pine nuts will be eaten and you will have a healthy new habit.

Habits can be hard to form, but if you do anything for a full lunar month, having invoked help from the Goddess, you will find it easier to stick to it. The bowl of pine nuts will help you see how far you've come as you go through the month.

A LIGHT SPELL

This spell helps us practice in the safety of our sacred space before venturing into the world. It is not so much a healing technique as an energizing one. The closer we come to understanding the powers we use, the less we need protection and the more we can become a source of spiritual energy for others.

You will need
- As many white candles as feels right (an odd number works well)
- Equivalent number of holders
- Anointing oil of frankincense

Method
Anoint the candles from middle to bottom then from middle to top. This is so you achieve a balance of physical and spiritual energy. Place the candles in the holders on the floor in a circle about six feet in diameter.

Standing in the circle, light the candles in a clockwise direction.

Stand in the center of the circle and "draw" the energy of the light toward you. Feel the energy as it seeps through your entire body, from your feet to your head.

Allow the energy to spill over from the crown of your head to fill the space around you. It should feel like a cocoon around your body. Now, visualize this cocoon of light gently radiating outward to the edge of your circle of candles.

When you feel ready, sit on the floor and allow the energy of the light to settle back inside you. Ground yourself by sweeping your body with your hands in the shape of the above figure, but do not lose the sense of increased energy.

Snuff out the candles in a clockwise direction, and use them only to repeat this technique until they are used up.

Gradually, as you become used to the sense of increased energy, you should find that you are more able to cope with difficulties and become more dynamic in the everyday world. It will become easier to carry the light inside you, not just inside the circle of candles, and you may find that you perceive more ways in which you can "help the world go around."

CERIDWEN'S SPELL

This spell pays homage to Ceridwen, a Welsh Goddess and nurturer of Taliesin, a Druidic Bard. She is invoked here, and asked for the gift of inspiration, called Awen by the Druids. This brings poetic inspiration, prophecy, and the ability to shape-shift (become something else). In bringing about change, this becomes a spell for creativity in all its forms. One of Ceridwen's symbols is the cauldron.

You will need

- Cauldron
- Seeds (preferably of wheat)
- White candle
- Incense made up of:
- I part rosebuds
- I part cedarwood chips
- I part sweet myrrh

Method

Blend your incense the night before you plan to use it.

Light your incense and the candle.

Place the cauldron in front of you and fill it up halfway with wheat seeds.

Stir the cauldron clockwise three times and let the seeds trickle through your fingers as you say:

Ceridwen, Ceridwen,
I seek your favor
Just as you searched for the
*   boy Gwion*
So I search for the power of Awen
Inspiration to be what I must,
to discover the known,
And to flow with change.
Grant, I pray, this power.

Since Awen is a threefold gift, you should repeat the stirring of the cauldron twice more or, alternatively, once on each of the following two days.

When you have finished, place the remains of the incense in the cauldron and bury the contents.

The candle may be snuffed out, but do not use it for anything else.

Ceridwen is said to have brewed herbs together to bring the gift of inspiration to her ugly son Agfaddu. Gwion was set to mind the potion but, in being splashed by the potion, absorbed its powers. In escaping the wrath of Ceridwen he became a seed of corn and was swallowed by her in the guise of a black hen. The Welsh bard Taliesin, born nine months later, was thus an initiated form of the boy. Artists, writers and poets can all seek this kind of inspiration.

CLEANSING THE AURA

This spell is a cleansing one that uses nothing but sound and can be done anywhere, although the open air is better. It will depend on your sense of yourself what sound you use, but the one here is known to be successful.

You will need
• An open space
• Your voice

Method
Find a spot in which you feel comfortable in your open space.

The choice of spot will depend on what you are attempting to get rid of. Be sure to take your time choosing, so it feels absolutely right. Settle yourself comfortably on the ground.

Take a big, deep breath and then exhale. Your exhalation should be slightly longer than your inhalation.

Do this three times to clear your lungs.

Now take a further deep breath and this time, as you exhale, say as loudly as you can:

Ahh... Ee... Oo...

Repeat the sounds at least twice more, increasing in intensity each time until you are actually screaming.

If you can, continue for two more sets of three (nine times in all, although six is fine.)

Finally, sit quietly, place your hands on the earth or the floor, reorient yourself in your surroundings, and absorb fresh energy.

Become aware of the sounds around you. Leave the area in silence, feeling the resonance of your sounds in the air.

This is a powerful technique, and you need to be quiet for the rest of the day so you can allow the energy to settle. The technique is a good way to deal with the frustrations of your everyday world, and it often results in being able to look at things from a different perspective.

DRAWING OUT A LATENT TALENT

This charm is to bring out an existing talent and develop a potential one, not give you one you don't already have. If you have a secret ambition, you might try this spell. It uses herbs as its vehicle, and could be done at the time of the Crescent Moon.

You will need
• A small drawstring bag about 3 inches

(10 cms) deep
- Liquorice root powder
- Rose hips
- Fennel
- Catnip
- Elderflower

Method

Put a pinch or two of the liquorice root, rose hips, fennel, catnip and elderflower in the bag. Then hang the bag outdoors at dusk.

At midnight, remove the bag and place it around your neck. If you like, you can make an affirmation before you go to sleep.

Say these words, or similar:

As I sleep, I shall learn of my best potential.

You must then wear the charm bag for a full 24 hours to allow the spell to work.

After that, place the charm bag under your pillow the night before anything important is to happen when you feel you need some extra help in reaching your goals.

Sleeping and dreaming are often the best way of self-development we have. Most of us have secret ambitions, but are prevented from succeeding by doubts. This spell helps make those fears irrelevant.

GOOD HEALTH WISHING SPELL

This spell is worked at the time of the New Moon, and is incredibly simple. Bay leaves possess a great deal of magical power and are used for granting wishes. This spell can be used to fulfill a range of desires; here, it is used to bring about health and happiness.

You will need
- 3 bay leaves
- Piece of paper
- Pencil or pen

Method

During a New Moon, write your wish on a piece of paper and visualize it coming true. Fold the paper into thirds, placing the three bay leaves inside. Fold the paper toward you.

Again visualize your wish coming true. Fold the paper into thirds a second time, thus forming an envelope.

Keep it hidden in a dark place. Reinforce your wish by repeatedly visualizing it coming true. When the wish comes true, burn the paper as a show of thanks.

This little envelope of power can also be included in a mojo or talisman bag to add power to it. In that case, be as specific as you can in your

wish. Using it this way, you may impose a time limit on the spell coming to fruition—but it is better not to do so.

OVERCOMING YOUR SHADOWS

This spell, which signifies letting go of the hurts of the past in a way that allows you to move forward with fresh energy, can be performed at the time of the New Moon. By carrying it out every New Moon, you are gradually able to cleanse yourself of the detritus of the past.

You will need
• Cedar or sage smudging stick or cleansing incense
• Bell
• Athame or ritual knife
• White candle
• Cakes and wine or juice

Method
Cast your circle by using the smudge stick or incense to "sweep" the space as you move around the circle clockwise.

Think of your space as being dome-shaped over your head, and cleanse that space too. Ring the bell. With your arms raised and your palms facing upward, acknowledge the Goddess and say:

Great Goddess,
Queen of the Underworld,
Protector of all believers in you,
It is my will on this night of the
new moon
To overcome my shadows and bring
about change.
I invite you to this, my circle, to assist
and protect me in my rite.

Hold your athame or knife in your hands in acknowledgment of the God and say:

Great God,
Lord of the Upper realms,
Friend of all who work with you,
It is my will on this night of the
new moon
To overcome my shadows to bring
about change.
I invite you to my circle to assist me
and protect me in my rite.

Light the candle and say:

Behind me the darkness, in front of
me the light
As the wheel turns,
I know that every end is a beginning.
I see birth, death and regeneration.

Spend a little time in quiet thought. If you can remember a time—either in the last month, or previously—when times have not been good for you, concentrate on that.

While the candle begins to burn, remember what that time felt like.

Now concentrate on the flame and allow yourself to feel the positivity of the light. Pick up the candle and hold it high above your head.

Feel the energy of the light shower down around you, and the negativity drain away.

Now draw the power of the light into you and feel the energy flowing through you.

Pass the candle around you and visualize the energy building up. If you wish, say:

Let the light cast out darkness.

Now ground yourself by partaking of the food and drink. Thank the God and Goddess for their presence. Withdraw the circle.

This is a personal way for you to acknowledge the God and Goddess in your everyday life. While on first acquaintance it appears to be a protection technique, it is actually one to enhance your energies and to allow you to be healthy and happy in all levels of existence.

PURIFYING EMOTIONS

This spell is one that helps you release negativity and distress that build up when you don't feel in control of your life. It uses the four Elements and may be performed on any evening during a waning Moon. It has deliberately been kept simple so you can spend more time learning how to make your emotions work for you rather than letting them overwhelm you.

You will need
- White candle
- Bowl of water
- Bowl of salt
- Dried herbs (such as sage for wisdom)
- Vessel in which the herbs can be burned

Method
Stand in your sacred space, light the candle and say:

> *I call upon the Elements*
> *in this simple ceremony*
> *that I may be cleansed from the*
> *contamination of negativity.*

Wave your hand quickly over or through the flame and say:

I willingly release negative action in my fire.

Rub the salt on your hands and say:

I release stumbling blocks and obstacles in my earth.

Put the herbs in the container and light them. Wave the smoke in front of you, inhale the perfume as it burns, and say:

I clear my air of unwise thoughts.

Dip your hands in the water and say:

*I purify this water.
Let this relinquishing be gentle.
Purified, cleansed and released in all ways,
I now acknowledge my trust and faith in my own clarity.*

Spend a little time thinking about the weeks to come.

Recognize that there may be times when you need the clarity you have just requested.

Now dispose of the ingredients immediately in the following way:

Put the salt in with the ashes, then pour the water on the ground so it mingles with the ashes and salt.

It can be helpful to find some sort of ceremonial way of releasing energy that enables you to let go of an old situation that's troubling you. A good time to do this is just before a New Moon, so you can begin a fresh cycle with renewed vigor.

THE SPELL OF THE SHELL

This is a lunar spell that calls on the power of the Moon and the waves. It is also representational, because the shell is a long accepted symbol for the Goddess and signifies her ability to take all things to her and effect changes. You can use this spell for healing if you choose a symbol that means this for you; otherwise, it can be used for other purposes. It is performed at the seaside.

You will need
• Shell
• A symbol of your desire
• Fine-nibbed marker

Method

To perform this spell, find a shell in shallow water.

Dry the shell thoroughly, and draw your chosen symbol on it. Place it on the shore so the tide will bring the waves across it. When the shell is in place, draw a triangle in the sand, enclosing the shell.

The symbol on the shell must be facing upward (towards the Moon). Meaningful words or phrases can also be placed on the shell, or simply written in the sand (inside the triangle).

Finally, face the Moon and say the following words of enchantment:

Goddess of Moon, Earth and Sea,
Each wish in thy name must
*   come to be.*
Powers and forces which tides
*   do make,*
Now summon thy waves, my spell to
take.

Leave the area now and the spell is set. Once the waves come, your wish will be taken out to the spirits of the sea.

It will usually take about seven days for a lunar spell to begin to manifest, but it can take as long as 28 days.

This type of magic is what we called "little works;" it belongs to the folk-magic level of spell-making. Take care to note the phase of the Moon (waxing to gain something, waning to dissolve something). You are using natural objects that, to the uninitiated, mean nothing. This means that these spells can be performed discreetly.

BALANCING YOUR ENERGIES

This spell principally uses the energy of the earth and of candles. The spell can be performed during the day if you particularly appreciate the light, or at night when you honor the Moon. It is good to perform it outside, as an appreciation of energy returning to the earth.

You will need
- Fresh flowers for your sacred space
- Single white flower
- Bowl of water large enough to hold the flower
- Green and yellow candles
- Jasmine or rose incense

Method
Prepare your sacred space as usual, making sure to use plenty of fresh flowers. Float the single white flower in the bowl of water,

thinking all the time of its beauty.

Light the candles, thinking all the while of the freshness of Mother Nature's energies.

Light the incense, and become aware of the perfumes created. Quietly consider the cycle and power of Nature.

Stand with your feet about 18 inches apart.

Become aware of your connection with the earth, mentally reaching toward its center through the soles of your feet.

Feel the energy rising through you toward the light. Reach toward the light and feel its energy moving downward through you.

Let those energies mingle with those of the earth. Allow the new energies to swirl around and through you, cleansing, healing and balancing. Say:

Lady of flowers and strong new life
Be born anew in me tonight.

When you feel refreshed, ground yourself by running your hands over your body from head to toe. Sit quietly for a short while and contemplate how you will use your new energy. Finally, allow your energy to settle in your solar plexus.

This spell is designed to replace old, stale energy with new vital force. You should come away feeling refreshed and invigorated. While this spell has similarities to rituals to Ostara, the single white flower also represents the Moon and therefore feminine energy.

ISIS GIRDLE

This spell is based on knot magic, and is used to ensure that your energy is at the right level for your magical work. Buckles, belts or girdles were often associated with Isis or Venus, and therefore aspects of femininity. They represent physical wellbeing and moral strength. It can be performed on a Wednesday during any Moon phase.

You will need
• 3 lengths of cord, each about 9 feet (3 meters) long

Method
Before you begin, decide on the purpose of your girdle. To use one specifically for health issues, you might choose the color blue; to work from a spiritual perspective, choose purple or white.

Start braiding the cord, and as you do so keep in mind that you are fashioning three

aspects of self—body, mind and spirit—to become one source of power in all that you do. That way, the braid becomes an extension of you and a protector of your being. Call on the power of Isis to give you strength and determination.

Tie a knot at both ends to tie in the power. Now consecrate the girdle by holding it in your left hand and circling it three times counterclockwise with your most powerful hand, while saying words such as:

Isis, Mistress of the words of power
Cleanse this girdle for my use

Visualize it surrounded by bright light, and glowing brightly. Let the image fade.

Next, circle the girdle clockwise three times with your power hand and say:

Isis, Goddess of the Throne
Protect me from all ill

Again visualize the girdle surrounded by light. Next, put the girdle around your waist and say:

Isis, Goddess of Perceived Truth
Thy wisdom is reality

This time, feel the energy pulsating in the girdle and say:

I stand ready to do thy work

In the future, every time you put on the girdle you should be able to sense the energy, giving you the power to carry out your chosen task.

This is quite a powerful spell. It not only protects you from illness, it also prepares you to be able to help others. Since Isis rules intuition, you'll find that you are in a better position to understand others' pain and distress.

KNOT SPELL

To get rid of a problem or a troublesome situation, you can use a representation of the problem in a tangled and knotted length of yarn. There are different ways of getting rid of the problem. This spell is in two parts, and is best done at the time of the Full Moon.

You will need
- Biodegradable string or cotton yarn
- Ingredients for a ritual bath (including candles and a purification oil)
- Three candles: one in your astrological

color, one dark or black (to represent negativity), and one white (to signify a life without problems)

Method: PART ONE

Your string needs to be biodegradable to reinforce the idea that your problems will dissolve.

The string or yarn can be in the appropriate color for the problem to be solved (green for money, red for love, etc.).

Sit quietly and think of all your fears and problems. Let them pass into the yarn.

Tie the yarn in knots to symbolize how mixed-up your problems make you feel.

One way of dealing with your difficulties is to take the knotted yarn to a high place and let the wind blow it away, along with your negativity.

Another way is to bury the yarn in soft ground, although this method will mean that the resolution of your problems may come slowly.

A third way is to begin to untie the knots and, as you do so, ask for help in seeing and understanding solutions.

This last method does not have to be done all at once; it can be done over time.

Method: PART TWO

Whichever method you use, make sure you take a ritual bath or shower cleansing after working with the string.

Anoint the candles with a purification or blessing oil. Anoint the dark candle from the end to the wick to remove bad luck. The others are done from the wick to the end to bring you what you desire. Have your ritual bath as usual.

This spell has two parts: first getting rid of the problems, then cleansing yourself of their effects. Only then can you decide how you are going to make changes in your life so you don't attract more problems.

MARS WATER

Water charged with iron was at one time considered to be a healing potion, and a way of treating anemia. Today it is considered a protective device and, when you feel under attack, it can enable you to send a curse or hex back to where it belongs.

You will need
• Iron nails or filings
• Large jar with lid
• Enough water to cover the nails

Method

Put the nails or filings in the jar and cover them with water.

Close the jar and leave it undisturbed until rust begins to form. The jar can be opened occasionally to check on its condition, which helps the formation of rust. This should take seven to ten days.

After this time, the jar may be shaken and the water strained and used as appropriate. Keep adding water to the jar as necessary to maintain its potency. You should not need to renew the nails unless the concoction begins to develop mold, in which case throw everything out and start again. When using the water, you may like to acknowledge Mars by using words such as:

> *Mars, God of War protect me now as*
> *I [state task]*

You can use some of the water in your ritual bath to cleanse and empower your hands before an important event. A business situation that required you to be more than usually aggressive might need a crystal charged in Mars water to make it especially powerful.

SELF-ESTEEM

This spell uses visualization, candles, cord and color, and requires very little effort, although it takes a week. It is a spell that men can do very easily, and can see and feel tangible results. It affects self-esteem and virility.

You will need
• 7 lengths of string or cord, each about 6 inches long
• 7 tea lights
• 7 small squares of red paper or cloth

Method
On returning from work, place a tea light on one red square. Surround the tea light with a piece of cord, placing it on a red square. As you do this say:

> *This represents me and all I feel*
> *myself to be*
> *I wish to be [strong, virile, at ease*
> *with myself—your choice of words]*

Let the tea light burn out. The next morning, knot both ends of the string or cord while saying:

*This cord carries my intent to be
[your choice of words]*

Carry the cord with you, and when you need to, throughout the day, remind yourself of your intent. Repeat the procedure for seven nights using the same words and either the same intent or another one that feels more appropriate. Repeat the same procedure as the first morning also.

At the end of the seven days, either tie the cords together in one loop (end to end) or tie them so they form a tassel. Either way, hang them by your mirror, where you are sure to see them. Each morning for about six weeks, choose which affirmation you wish to use that day, and make sure you have acted accordingly.

This spell has a long-term effect on your personality. Each time you make the morning affirmation, you are calling on the power of the whole to assist you in being the kind of person you want to be. Any behavior that does not fit that image soon drops away.

TO FIND THE TRUTH

Without the truth, one cannot make sensible decisions. As one's intuition grows, it becomes easier to tell when people are not telling you the truth. Until that time, a simple spell like this ensures that the truth is revealed in the right way. It uses herbs and candles.

You will need
- Handful of thyme
- Red candle
- Flat dish or pentacle on which to put the herbs

Method
Place the thyme into the dish and say:

> *Clarification I now require
> So that truth is spoken
> Let what is hidden now
> Be brought into the open.*

Light the candle and say:

> *Speak truth with passion
> And goodbye to caution
> As the truth is said
> May I not be misled.*

Allow the candle to burn down until the wax drips into the herbs.

Bury the cooled wax and herbs, preferably at a crossroads, having first blown any loose herbs to the wind.

Thyme is said to bring courage, which is often needed to bypass our inhibitions. The color red often represents sexual passion, but here it is more about the passion for truth. Remember that sometimes the truth can hurt, and you may have been being protected.

TO SLOW DOWN A SITUATION

When things are happening too fast and we feel that life is running away with us, it is possible to slow things down. For this, we use the power of Saturn and his control of time, coupled with the idea that if something is frozen, it allows us time to think and consider our actions.

You will need
- Paper
- Black pen and ink
- Your freezer

Method
On the front of the paper write a few words about, or draw a representation of, the situation you feel is moving too fast.

On the back of the paper, draw the symbol for Saturn.

♄

Put the paper into your freezer or ice compartment and leave it until you feel you can handle your problem again.

Tear the paper into small pieces and flush it away or burn it safely.

This spell uses the power of Saturn, the Roman god of Time and agriculture. By using the freezer, we are bringing this spell up to date and utilizing the idea of solidifying something rather than allowing it to flow.

RE-ENCHANTING THE WORLD RITUAL

When you have demands on your time and energy, it's easy to forget about ritual and spell-work. Suddenly you have no idea what phase the moon is in, and it has been weeks since you did anything magical. This is the time to stop and rebalance yourself. The dense energy of the world is clinging to you and weighing you down.

Begin by decluttering your physical space. Turn off the TV or radio, and disengage from social media. This will help you reconnect to your own intuition rather than be buffeted by the opinions of others.

After you declutter, visualize a golden, sparkling energy coming in through your front door (even if it is closed) and

whooshing around your home, clearing away anything that isn't meant to be there. Then do this prayer on a waxing Moon.

You will need
• White or gold candle

Method
Sit where you won't be disturbed for a while. Light the candle. Close your eyes and place your hands, palms facing upwards, beside you or in your lap.

Call on the god or goddess you most affiliate with to guide you. Ask what you should do to make your experience of life more magical.

Sit in this space for a while, thinking about the answers you are being given. Then turn your palms downward and rub them against your legs and open your eyes.

Write down the answers you've been given.

Review your answers two weeks later and see how they relate to what has happened.

Now that you have opened the doors of communication with your divine guide, you will also find that you receive powerful, transforming dreams and experience strange, delightful coincidences.

This ritual or prayer asks for help from the divine to access a place of inspiration in your life and to beat everyday blues. However, another vital cure for feelings of disconnection is to get out in nature. Dragonflies become fairies in disguise. Trees speak to you in rustling voices. That rabbit that darts across your path has a message for you, as does the fox following swiftly behind it. Brother Crow wants you to be happy. And spending time with all these elements might just get you there.

THE EVIL EYE

The evil eye is an ancient and deeply held belief in more than one third of the world's cultures; it is particularly prominent in the Mediterranean and in Celtic countries.

DIAGNOSIS OF THE EVIL EYE

You will need
- Olive oil
- Bowl of water

Method
Drip three drops of olive oil on the surface of the water. Watch what happens.

If the drops remain distinct, there is no evil eye. If they run together, there is.

Dispose of the oil and water safely.

There are many ways of removing the evil eye. The following is just one method.

REMOVAL OF THE EVIL EYE

You will need
- Lemon
- Iron nails

Method
Using some force, drive the nails into the lemon. Visualize the evil eye being pierced.

Keep the lemon for three days, by which time it should begin to rot.

If it does not, repeat the procedure.

Here you have externalized the difficulty, checked that the spell worked and repeated the procedure if not. You could then repeat the diagnostic procedure to ensure that you are clear.

The Greek Orthodox Church forbids people to go to "readers" or other individuals for use of magical rituals to overcome the evil eye. It is stated quite categorically that such people take advantage of the weakness of superstitious people and destroy them spiritually and financially by playing upon their imagination. However, Vaskania—which is another word for the evil eye—is recognized simply as a phenomenon that was accepted as fact. It is the jealousy and envy of some people for things they do not possess, such as beauty, youth or courage. Though the Church rejected Vaskania as contradicting divine providence, the prayers of the Church to avert the evil eye are an implicit acceptance of its existence.

In Scotland, it seems that the evil eye was more often associated with women—and therefore with the crone, or wise woman—than with men. Anyone with a squint or

eyes of different colors could be accused of possessing the evil eye, and of using it to cause harm or illness. A charmed burrach or cow fetter could be used to protect animals. Other preventative measures could also be taken, some using plants and trees—such as rowan and juniper—and others using horseshoes and iron stakes.

SALT METHOD FOR REMOVAL OF EVIL EYE

You can also remove the evil eye with sea salt. It is placed on your altar and consecrated as "goddess salt"—the culmination of your prayers to the goddess and your meditations at your altar. Remember to keep the salt on your altar for a lunar month before using it.

You will need
• A bowl of sea salt

Method
Having consecrated your sea salt and placed it on your altar, you should end every working with a short request to the goddess that she imbue the salt with her protective qualities.

After one lunar month, your salt will be ready for use in the removal of the evil eye.

Simply say a prayer of gratitude to the goddess whenever you need the remedy, and take a few grains of the salt and put it in the mouth of whoever needs it.

Note that the salt can be used in a variety of remedies, including for healing and for protection. It is not just for the evil eye.

Avoid accidentally giving anyone else the evil eye by not envying anyone and always saying "bless him/her/them" whenever you praise them or something they have. This simply lets the Universe know that you intend them no harm and that you have their best interests at heart. In some cultures, it is considered poor form to compliment others without adding a blessing, as it is seen to attract the evil eye and a subsequent loss of the quality that you are praising.

MONEY, LUCK, AND CAREER

It might be easier to think of this section under the title of Resources. Most of us need—or at least imagine we need—more money, or the wherewithal to do more with our lives, and the spells in this section are designed to help you do just that. Mainly, they may help you move away from so-called "poverty mentality" and perhaps realize that you deserve to be rewarded for living according to your principles.

ATTRACTING EXTRA MONEY

This is a representational spell, since the money in your pocket is representative of greater fortune. Use this spell only at the time of a New Moon, and make sure you are in the open air. It is said that the spell is negated if the Moon is seen through glass.

You will need
• Loose change

Method
Gaze at the Moon. Turn your money over in your pocket. As you do so, repeat the following three times:

*Goddess of Light and Love, I pray
Bring fortune unto me this day.*

You will know it has worked when you find extra money in your pocket or purse, or come across some unexpectedly.

In previous times, the Moon was recognized as much as the Sun for bringing good luck. This spell acknowledges that, and allows you to make use of her power. It is said to ensure that you have at least enough for bed and board until the next New Moon.

FOOTWASH FOR MONEY

This is a folklore recipe, and would strictly only become a spell if an incantation or invocation were added. Black Cohosh, when used as a footwash, can lead you to money.

You will need
• Black Cohosh root
• Cup of boiling water
• Small bottle

Method

Soak the root in the cup of boiling water for 15 minutes. Strain the water and throw away the root. Put the liquid in the bottle for seven days and leave it alone.

On the eighth day, rub the liquid all over the bottom of your shoes.

Be alert to your own intuition until money comes your way.

It is said that you will find, win, or gain money in some legal manner. This, by its method, cannot really be used to gain a specific amount, but you can keep in mind what your needs are.

HOW TO SPEED UP A HAPPENING

Sometimes we find ourselves in a situation that is not happening quickly enough for us, such as a business deal or house purchase.

We can use our knowledge of color, herbs and spices to speed things up. We may not always know what circumstances surround the problem, so it is wise to keep in mind the words "if it be right" or "An it harm no-one."

You will need
- Red candle
- Fast luck incense
- Cinnamon powder

- Papers associated with, or representative of, the issue

Method

Sprinkle each of the papers with cinnamon powder. Arrange in a pile. Place the candle on top of the papers.

As you do this, repeat the following words three times:

> *Time passed, time fast*
> *Let this [event] happen*

Light the incense and the candle, and allow them to burn out.

When doing this spell, be sure to keep a close eye on the candle so that the papers are never in danger of burning.

A MAGICAL POMANDER

As our knowledge of herbs and magic increases, we can use old-fashioned ideas and charming customs, and perhaps return them to their original use. Pomanders—aromatic spheres that are prepared by studding oranges with cloves—have been used since medieval times to keep odors at bay. Magically, they can be used to attract money, for protection, and—when they

have lost their fragrance—as an offering through fire to the gods.

You will need
- An orange with an oily skin
- A nail or knitting needle
- A good quantity of whole cloves
- Cinnamon powder
- Plastic bag
- Ribbon
- Pins

Method
Stud the orange with whole cloves, complete with stems, bud side out. It is easier to insert the cloves if you first poke a small hole with the nail or knitting needle. Space the cloves evenly in a pattern that pleases you, leaving room to tie the ribbon. The cloves will move closer together as the orange dries out. Keep your intent for the pomander in mind.

Place the powdered cinnamon in the plastic bag, and shake the pomander inside the bag until it is well coated with the powder.

Leave in a warm place to dry out, which may take up to six weeks.

Check frequently that the orange is not getting moldy, but try not to open the bag.

Finally, tie the ribbon around the pomander, fixing it securely with the pins.

Hang the pomander where you can see it and enjoy the fragrance.

When it's time to dispose of the pomander, throw it into a fire. Say:

As I return this to its Element
Sun, Jupiter, Venus
I thank you for your help.

Made in this way, the pomander can last up to a year before its fragrance disappears.

This pomander is multipurpose. All the components are ruled by the element of Fire, and the relevant deities and planetary influences are Sun for the orange, Jupiter for the cloves and Venus for the cinnamon.

ACHIEVING A DREAM JOB

Candles often work well when dealing with aims and aspirations. This spell introduces some of the techniques beloved of those who believe in using the Element of Fire, which represents drive. This particular spell is best begun on the night of a New Moon.

You will need
- 2 brown candles (to represent the job)
- Green candle (for prosperity)

- A candle to represent yourself (perhaps your astrological color)
- Prosperity incense, such as cinnamon
- Prosperity oil such as bergamot or blended patchouli and basil

Method

Light your prosperity incense. Anoint the candles with the prosperity oil from wick to end, since you want good things to come toward you.

Place one of the brown candles in the center of your space.

Place the green one on the right, with your personal candle on the left. (These candles should be in a safe place; they have to burn out entirely.) As you light your personal candle, say:

Open the way, clear my sight.
Bring me chance, that is my right.

Light the green candle and say:

Good luck is mine and true victory,
Help me Great Ones, come to me.

Light the brown candle and say:

Openings, work, rewards I see,
And as I will, So Must it Be.

Leave the candles to burn out completely.

Each night for a week—or until the candle is used up—light the second brown candle for 9 minutes while contemplating the job and the good to come out of it.

You should identify exactly what you mean by "dream job." It is of little use to aim for something that is beyond your capabilities, although you might wish for one that will eventually take you to where you want to be.

ACTIVATING A WISH

It is easy to categorize the granting of wishes as a separate area of spell-making but, depending on the offering you make, it could be classified as crystal, candle, herbal or symbolic.

You will need

- Your chosen gift to the Elements, spirits or deities (this might be a crystal, plant, rune or piece of metal)
- A suitable place to make the offering (perhaps the woods, a stream, a high place or, in urban areas, a park, waterway or tall building)

Method

Before you begin, you need to give some thought to your wish.

Be specific in stating what you want; otherwise you might get more than you bargained for.

State your wish as clearly and briefly as possible, addressing your deity or spirit by name or title if you can, for instance:

> *Pan and spirits of the woodland*
> *Hear now my request*
> *I wish for health, love and happiness*
> *For [name]*

When you make your offering, be appropriate. For example:

If your wish is for material goods or money, you could use a crystal or coin and bury it to signify the tangibility of your desire.

If your wish has an emotional component, you might throw your offering into running water.

If your wish is for knowledge or information, signify this by going to a high place and using the currents of air.

You might, for instance, choose to scatter some plant seeds to help restore the ecological balance.

If you use the Element of Fire, be responsible. Use only dead wood and never place your fire close to plants or buildings.

Repeat your wish three times; any negativity attached to your desire should have dropped away by the third request. By then you will also be more aware of your own feelings, and whether you really want what you are asking for.

Making wishes is a quick way of making things happen in your everyday life, often without having to carry out a full-blown ceremony. As you get to know your own capabilities, you will be able to take advantage of the moments that are presented to you.

FOR STUDY AND CONCENTRATION

It is sometimes important to go back to basics to get the help we need. This is an herbal and color formula spell which also calls on the powers of Bridget, the goddess of poetry, or on Sarasvati, the goddess of knowledge. Your sachet will be purple for the former and white for the latter.

You will need

- 2 parts rosemary
- 2 parts basil
- 1 part caraway seeds

- 1 part dried rind of citrus fruit
- (a part equals one quantity)
- Small bowl to mix the herbs
- Small cloth bag about 6 inches (15 cms) deep
- Silver thread or cord

Method
Combine the herbs thoroughly while chanting either:

Bridget, Brighde fashioner of words,
Help me now as I seek your aid
Let me now bring you honor
In what I have to say today.

Or, for Sarasvati:

Sarasvati, divine consort of Brahma
Mistress of knowledge
Teach me to use words wisely and well
My doubts and fears I pray you dispel.

Now put the herbs in the bag, tying it securely with the silver cord. Place the sachet somewhere in your work area, where you can see it.

You should find that, simply by focusing on the sachet, you are able to free your mind from distractions and find inspiration as you study for tests or write your articles and masterpieces. If you become really stuck, pick up the sachet and allow some of the fragrance to escape. Tie it up again when you are finished.

MONEY CHARM

This is more of a charm than a spell because you have formed a different object (the bag) and given it power through incantation. As always, a money charm like this relies on the energy set up between you and the money. If you recognize that money is a resource, you can adjust the spell to ask for resources rather than money itself.

You will need
- A square of green cloth
- Allspice, borage, lavender and saffron
- Crystals (such as garnet, ruby, emerald or rock salt)
- Three silver coins
- Gold and silver-colored thread

Method
Hold the three silver coins in your hands.
Breathe on them four times and say:

To the spirits of Air I say
bring some money my way.

Put the herbs, crystals and coins on the cloth. Tie the cloth into a bag, using eight knots in the thread. (It is probably easiest to fold the thread into two and tie knots around the neck of the bag.)

Hide the bag in a safe, cool, dark place, away from prying eyes for eight days. After eight days, money should be coming in.

Be as realistic as possible, imagining what you will do with the money and how it will be used. Once you have made the bag, meditate daily on what you want. By using the three silver coins and four breaths you create the vibration of the number seven, which is considered a lucky and spiritual number.

REMOVING MISFORTUNE

This spell uses plant magic combined with folk magic and the meaning of numbers. Burying an object binds the energy of what it represents, and reciting prayers raises the vibration to the point where any negativity is nullified. The instruction "Within sight of a church" suggests that the bad luck is overseen by the Angels.

You will need
- 3 small jars (those from honey or baby food work well)
- 9 cloves of garlic
- 9 thorns from a white rose or 9 pins

Method
Pierce the garlic cloves with the pins or thorns, saying forcefully while doing so:

Misfortune begone from me.

Put three of the cloves and pins in each jar. Bury each jar within sight of a church. Say the Lord's Prayer each time you do this.

Walk away and don't look back at what you have done.

This spell can give impressively fast results. As soon as you become aware of the misfortune you are suffering, look for a common theme—i.e. whether the problems are financial, romantic, etc.—and name them in the words you use. Because you have addressed it three times, it cannot remain.

WANT SPELL

Since Mother Nature supplies our most basic needs, this spell uses the cycle of her existence to help fulfill your wants. The leaf is representative of her power, and you are using natural objects to signify that all things must come to pass.

You will need
- A marker
- A fully grown leaf

Method
One the leaf, write or draw a word, picture or letter that represents the thing you want.

Place the leaf on the ground.

As the leaf withers, it takes your desire to the Earth. In thanks, Mother Nature will grant your wish.

You may also throw the leaf into running water or place it under a stone.

This spell owes a great deal to folk magic and an appreciation of the cycle of growth and decay. In such spells, it is usual to use a leaf that has fallen rather than pick one from a tree. If you do the latter, you should thank the tree for its bounty.

TO CREATE OPPORTUNITY

This spell appeals to the Roman goddess Ops, who used to be petitioned by sitting down and touching the Earth with one hand, since she was a deity of prosperity, crops and fertility. During the Full Moon, using sympathetic magic, a wish doll representing health and happiness is made to draw opportunities toward you.

You will need
- A bowl of sand (to represent the earth)
- Green cloth
- Needle and thread
- Pen
- Cinnamon or cedar incense
- Dried chamomile, vervain or squill
- Mint and honeysuckle oil

Method
Make a doll out of the cloth. While concentrating on the opportunities available to you, write your name on the doll and stuff it with dried herbs that have had a few drops of the oils added. Sew the figure shut. Light the incense.

Hold the doll in the incense smoke. Say:

Goddess of opportunity,
Bring good fortune now to me
Guide me by your gentle hand
For I am as worthy as these grains
*   of sand.*

Let the sand trickle through your fingers to signify touching the earth.

Repeat this an odd number of times (seven works well).

Keep your doll safe. You do not have to have it with you at all times, just with your possessions or papers.

For the spell to continue to work, renew it every Full Moon.

This is a good spell to use for business opportunities, since the doll can be kept discreetly in a drawer or cupboard, and hopefully will become imbued with the excitement of your day-to-day work. It can also be used when you wish to enhance your career prospects.

TO HELP MAKE A DECISION

This spell uses color and candles to allow you to make a decision about two opposing outcomes. You are in a sense taking the dilemma to the highest authority in order for the best outcome to become apparent. Do the spell at the time of the New Moon if there is a new beginning involved.

You will need
- 2 yellow candles
- White candle or your astrological candle
- Length of purple ribbon just over half a yard long
- 2 pieces of paper
- Pen

Method
This spell takes three days to do in total.

Place the white candle in the middle of the ribbon. This ribbon signifies the highest possible spiritually correct energy. Place the two yellow candles on either end of the ribbon.

Write the two possible outcomes on the pieces of paper and fold them separately. Place the two papers under the yellow candles on top of the ribbon.

Light the middle (white) candle first and then the two outer (yellow) ones.

Acknowledge the fact that you will be extinguishing them as part of the spell.

Burn the candles for at least an hour, so a link is properly made. Consider both decisions carefully.

Snuff the candles out, and the next day move the papers and the outer candles closer to the middle candle. Roll the ribbon in toward the center against the candle bases.

Relight the candles and again burn them for at least an hour, considering your two options carefully.

Repeat each day until all the candles are grouped together. (This should take at least three days, and, if time allows, longer.)

Ensure that you have at least an hour's burning time left for the final day.

Allow the candles to burn out, and within three days you should find it easy to make a decision.

This process allows due consideration of the pros and cons of each option. It provides the energy for the correct decision and allows you to be rational and objective while still taking account of the emotional aspect. It keeps your mind focused on the matter at hand. You do not then "stand in your own light" (get in the way of your own success).

TO IMPROVE WORK RELATIONSHIPS

This is a combination candle and mirror spell, and is designed to improve the work environment. It works equally well for all levels of work relationship. Often, spells about work are best done at home, and a reminder taken in to reinforce it. The spell is carried out for seven days, and reinforced once a week. Tuesday or Thursday are good days.

You will need
- Small mirror that will fit unobtrusively in your drawer
- White candle
- Oil such as jasmine for spiritual love, or ylang ylang for balance

Method
Anoint the candle. Light the candle and burn it for at least an hour.

Concentrate for a few minutes on the image of your boss or colleague when they annoy you.

Look in the mirror and visualize them being pleasant and calm. See yourself working with them as an efficient team.

Do this each evening for a week, then do it once a week for at least six weeks.

During that time, keep the mirror in your work desk drawer and reinforce the positive visualization of your colleague or boss being calm every day.

You should see an improvement after a week; others may also notice a change as time goes on. As you become less stressed, you may find that you become more creative and are able deal with other petty annoyances.

WEAVING SUCCESS

The use of ribbons is an extension of knot magic, and is often used in binding or protection spells. However, this one is an unobtrusive way of enhancing the energy of your business as well as ensuring its security. Braiding three strands links us with the triple-aspected Great Mother— Maid, Mother, Crone.

You will need
• 3 equal lengths of ribbon: dark blue for success in long-term plans and clarity; yellow for mental power, wealth, communication and travel; and brown for grounding, stability, and endurance
• Large safety pin

Method
Pin the three ribbons together at the top to make braiding easier.

Braid them and, as you do, repeat the following words as often as you feel is right, remembering the significances of the colors:

> *Great Mother Great Mother*
> *Come to me now*
> *As these strands weave and*
>   *become one*
> *May this business grow*

Now loop the braid around your front-door handle so that anyone who comes into the business must pass it.

You should find that the qualities you have woven into the business begin to bring results quickly. Different color combinations will yield different results: red will bring vitality and willpower; orange success and prosperity through creativity; and yellow communication, mental power and wealth.

BAY LEAVES OF PROSPERITY

Bay leaves are traditionally plants of wealth and luck. If you are lucky enough to have a bay tree, you may experience good luck around money. However, even bay leaves bought at a supermarket have the potential to be powerful allies in your quest for financial success.

You will need
• 3 bay leaves
• Gold pen
• Gold candle

Method
Light the candle and sit in meditation for a while in front of it while thinking about why you want more money. Money is simply a medium of exchange, so what you do want to exchange that money for? Perhaps it's a feeling you'd like to experience, such as financial freedom or an end to worry.

Whatever it is, think deeply about it for some time as the gold candle burns. Then, taking the gold pen, write your name and the amount of money you wish to attract on each leaf. Carefully place all three leaves

in your wallet and wait patiently. When the money comes to you, give thanks to the Universe for its bounty, and bury the leaves in your yard or a window box. Try to keep the leaves in your possession as they break down.

If this spell works particularly well for you, it will be enhanced if you buy yourself a bay tree and put it at your front door or toward the front of your home, on a balcony.

GRAINS OF WEALTH

Grain has been used in harvest festivals to denote prosperity and good living for millennia.

You will need
- Bag of grain, such as wheat or spelt
- Large scarf or cloth
- Green candle
- Length of green ribbon or string

Method
Light the candle on your altar. It is important that you use a green candle, as it indicates to the Universe that this is a wealth spell. Put the cloth on your lap (sit on a chair or, if possible, the floor, with your legs crossed, so the cloth forms a receptacle). Taking a handful of the grains in your right hand, slowly pour them onto the cloth while saying:

Richest of grains, hear my plea
Give me the means to set myself free

Do this two more times so you have three handfuls of grain in the cloth on your lap. Bring the corners of the cloth together so it forms a pouch. Tie the top with the ribbon or string. Put the pouch of grains in a safe place and tap it on your resumé or any business-loan applications. You should see success as soon as it is right for you to have it.

You can substitute the grains with lentils or rice if your prefer. Ideally, it should be a grain you eat regularly.

CINNAMON CAKE SPELL

Cinnamon has long been associated with abundance and wealth. It is ruled by the Element Fire, which makes it good for fast-working spells. It's delicious, too.

You will need
- Your favorite basic cake recipe
- Cinnamon powder
- Cinnamon stick

Method

When you have the cake batter ready, sprinkle a teaspoon of cinnamon into the bowl, saying:

Fire spice, Fire spice,
wealth and love are in your gift
Let all who eat feel your bounty
So mote it be

Stir in the cinnamon with the cinnamon stick clockwise three times. Then bake the cake. Once it has cooled, cut a slice for your ancestors and place it on your altar. This portion should not be consumed, but put outdoors, for the birds, after 24 hours.

Slice the cake and share it with members of your household. Think about where you want more abundance in your life as you eat the cake.

This is an enjoyable spell, because it is as much a nourishing blessing as it is a ritual for bringing more prosperity into your life.

PEARL MONEY MAGNET SPELL

Pearls have long been associated with wealth due to the difficulty of procuring a true (rather than cultured) pearl. This spell uses those associations to draw money to you like a magnet. The "pearl" essentially becomes a charm.

You will need
• Pearl, or a bead that looks like a pearl
• White candle
• Green candle
• Dish of sea salt

Method

Place the dish of sea salt on your altar and put the pearl or bead on top of it. Light and set the white candle to the right of your altar as you are facing it. Place the green candle to the left and light it.

Raise your arms above you to form a Y with your body. With your palms facing upward, imagine pure white light coming down from the heavens and entering your palms. Let that light pool at your hands until it is a sphere of pulsating light. Then place the light on the pearl in your dish. Say:

Goddess of light, She who is perfect
Bless this sphere with your
*   generosity*

When you have visualized the light merging with the pearl, bring your hands together and close the working by thanking the Goddess and letting the energy recede

back inside you. Try "Earthing" yourself for a while by walking barefoot around the room.

Keep the pearl in your bag or pocket so it's always with you. It will continue to work in the background, attracting money and new opportunities for wealth.

Pure energy work such as this requires a lot of work on yourself so you don't "leak" energy or leave yourself energetically vulnerable. Therefore, remember to do your ritual baths and close down your energy work by grounding yourself in some way. Even eating a carb-dense snack such as a piece of toast can help.

ANIMAL ALLY FOR BUSINESS SUCCESS

Shamans have known for millennia that there are spirits that can help us in our everyday lives. The greatest part of their work for a community was to commune with those spirits to bring back healing for the people who needed it. In the same way, you can "journey" to find animal allies that embody qualities that help your career. A Full Moon is a good time for this work.

You will need
- Shamanic drumming CD or an audio file of shamanic drumming
- Blanket
- Representational totem (see below)

Method
On the night of a Full Moon, lie down on your bed and state your intention for your journey; in this case, it could be something like, "I am journeying to meet my power animal, who can be an ally to me in my business life." Play the drumming music. Put the blanket over you so you feel warm as the journey continues. The drumming will lead you to the World Tree, in your imagination.

From there, you should journey down through the roots to get to the Lower World, where you can meet your power animal.

The animal you encounter may not be the one you thought you would find. You may have been thinking of a glamorous, fierce lion but instead meet a squirrel. It doesn't matter what the animal is; you should check that it shows you itself from three sides, ask it its name, and thank it for its help.

As the drumming changes to a higher tempo, return up through the sky of the Lower World, through the roots of the

tree, to our world. Finally, you should feel yourself back in your bed. Wiggle your toes and fingers to bring yourself back to the here and now. Sit up and drink a glass of water if you need it.

Having secured the help of a power animal, you should discover the message it has for you. That aforementioned squirrel might be a message for you to prepare for the winter by storing "nuts" (money and resources). It may be its wise counsel to prepare for leaner times. Researching the qualities and concerns of the animal that came to you can give meaning to the journey and to how you can gain help in your business life.

You should also try to find a small figurine of the animal to carry with you as a totem. If you can't find one, use a small stone to represent it, and keep it with you as you go about your day.

Animals can help us in our daily lives. They are more intuitive than humans, and often show great kindness. Keep an eye out for animal helpers in your daily life, and pay attention to their behaviors to see what you can learn from them.

FIGS AND HONEY SPELL

You can add figs to increase the potency of a spell using honey. The idea is to impress upon the world that you have the means to luxuriate in food items that would have been costly in times gone by and indicated a wealthy person.

You will need
- Plump, ripe fig
- Jar of honey
- Small plate

Method
Begin this spell by cutting the fig into slices, putting it on the plate, and drizzling it with honey. Put the plate on your altar. Then say:

Honeyed be this fig
And honeyed be my words
Sweetest success stick to me
And so mote it be

Eat the fig, giving thanks for all the bounty in your life. Doing this spell once a month is a good way of expressing gratitude for all you have, and inviting more to come.

BLESSED NUTMEG

Nutmeg was once an expensive commodity that people would keep with them to grate into their drinks. This spell uses the magical properties of this spice as a signifier of wealth and prosperity. It is done on a waxing Moon and is particularly good to do in winter.

You will need
- Nutmeg
- Nutmeg grater
- Green candle
- Nutmeg essential oil

Method
Anoint the candle with the nutmeg oil, moving from bottom to top. Light the candle on your altar, with the nutmeg and grater placed there too. Licking your right index finger (the finger of Jupiter), touch the nutmeg and say:

Blessings be upon this spice
Blessings be, wealth to entice

Place the nutmeg and grater in your bag or pocket. Next time you buy a coffee or a hot chocolate, grate a tiny bit of nutmeg onto it and think about how lucky you are. It is said that the more people think of themselves as lucky, the luckier they get.

The use of saliva in licking the finger and placing it on the nutmeg connects that particular nutmeg to you. Saliva is used in a number of traditions, as all bodily fluids tie magic to you personally and become a source of your power. If you dislike working with such substances, you can achieve a similar result by holding your Jupiter (index) finger to your belly button and imagining a ball of light emanating from there and sticking to your finger. Transfer that ball of light to the nutmeg.

HOME AND PERSONAL PROTECTION

Protection spells form an integral part of any spell-worker's armory. When you are working with powers that are not well understood, you can open yourself up to all sorts of negativity, and sometimes sheer goodwill is not enough to protect your personal space. Equally, as you develop your own abilities, it becomes possible to protect those around you from harm.

ANIMAL STONES

The ancients were very good at perceiving shapes in stones and wood, and believed that such shapes could be made to hold the spirit of the animal "trapped" in such a way. Many artists are still able to do this, and as magic makers we, too, can make use of this art. When on your wanderings you find an interesting stone or piece of driftwood, look at it with fresh eyes and turn it into a fetish—the correct meaning of which is an object that is believed to have magical or spiritual powers. Your fetish will help you as an ally and, over time, will become more powerful and connected to you.

You will need
- Pleasingly shaped stone or piece of wood
- Paints and brushes
- Decorations such as beads and ribbons
- Glue
- Incense such as benzoin or frankincense
- Small box

Method
Light the incense. Sit quietly with your object and let it "speak" to you.

Allow the ideas to flow as to what it might become—your totem animal, a bear, a horse or perhaps a dog or cat.

Decorate the object appropriately, taking care to enhance the natural shape rather than change it.

You can now consecrate it in one of two ways. Pass the object quickly through the smoke of the incense three times to empower it with the spirit of the animal.

Or
Place it in the box with an appropriate image or herbs, and bury it for three days or place it on your altar for the same amount

of time. This allows the metamorphosis to take place and the spirit of the animal to enter your now magical object.

It is now ready for use, perhaps to help you access the wisdom of the animals, as a healing device or for protection. Ancients believed that the fetish must be fed so it would retain its magical powers. Today, corn is an appropriate "food," as is pollen, although you can use your imagination, since it is your creation. If you do not feed (energize) it for a while, you might need to consecrate it again for it to work properly.

BLESSING FOR THE HEART OF THE HOME

This is a candle, crystal and representational spell that calls upon Hestia, goddess of the hearth and home, to bring her qualities of constancy, calm and gentleness to bear on your home. Hestia is supportive of the family and home, and was praised by the poet Homer in ancient Greece.

You will need
- Lavender candle
- Small silver or brass bowl in which to stand the candle
- Lavender flowers
- Small piece of amethyst

Method
Before placing the candle in the bowl, raise the latter above your head and say:

*Hestia, you who tends the holy house of the lord Apollo,
Draw near, and bestow grace upon my home.*

Place the candle in the bowl, making sure the candle will stand firmly. Light the candle, and when it is lit, pass the amethyst three times through the flame and say:

Hestia, glorious is your portion and your right.

Place the amethyst in your hearth or close to your fireplace. (If you have no fireplace, then as close to the center of your home as possible.) Sprinkle some of the lavender flowers in your doorway to keep your home safe. Say:

Hail Hestia, I will remember you.

Allow the candle to burn down, then place some of the lavender flowers in the bowl, leaving it in a safe space.

When the atmosphere in the home becomes

fraught, this spell can bring a period of peace and tranquility. The bowl, lavender flowers and amethyst are all sacred to Hestia, and remind you of her presence.

CLEANSING THE BODY OF NEGATIVE ENERGIES

This spell uses candle magic and an appeal to the Elements. One aspect needs to be noted: black candles were once associated with malevolence, but today are used in many different ways, some positive and some negative. This is an old spell, so the association with negativity remains, but you may use a dark blue candle if you prefer.

You will need
- White or yellow candle (for positive energy)
- Black or dark blue candle (for negative energy)
- Green candle (for healing)

Method
In your sacred space, place the candles in a triangle with the green candle closest to you. Clear your mind of everything except what you are doing.

Light the white candle, staying aware of its symbolism, and say:

Earth, Fire, Wind, Water and Spirit; I ask thee to cleanse my body of all negative energies.

Light the black or blue candle, also keeping aware of its symbolism.

Repeat the words above, and pause to let the energies come to a natural balance.

Light the green candle, and again repeat the above words.

Sit back, keep your mind clear, and be peaceful for at least 10 minutes.

When the time feels right, either snuff out the candles or allow the green one to burn all the way down, so you are filled with healing energy.

You should feel rested and relaxed, and more ready to tackle problems as they arise. Make this part of your weekly routine until you feel it is no longer necessary.

TO REVERSE NEGATIVITY OR HEXES

Try this candle spell using the element of Fire to reverse any negativity or hexes you become aware of being sent in your direction. Anger from others can often be dealt with in this way, but deliberate maliciousness may require more force. You

need to be as dispassionate as you can when dealing with a hex, which is defined as "an evil spell."

You will need
- Purple candle
- Rosemary oil
- White paper
- Black ink
- Fireproof dish such as your cauldron or an ashtray

Method
Visualize all blocks in your life-path being removed. Anoint your candle with the oil.

On the piece of paper, write in black ink:

All blocks are now removed.

Fold the paper three times, away from you.

Light the candle and burn the paper in your dish.

Invoke the power of Fire and its Elemental spirits by repeating three times:

Firedrakes and salamanders,
Aid me in my quest,
Protect me from all evil thoughts
Turn away and send back this hex.

After the third repetition, close the spell in whatever way is appropriate for you.

A simple statement is enough:

Let it be so.

No one has the right to curse or malign another person, and all you are doing with this spell is turning the negativity back where it belongs. When you use the power of Fire, you are harnessing one of the most potent forces of the universe, so be sure you use it wisely and well.

HOUSEHOLD GODS

Household gods are found in most folk religions. In Rome, the penates were household gods, primarily guardians of the storeroom. They were worshipped in connection with the lares, beneficent spirits of ancestors, and, as guardians of the hearth, with Vesta or Hestia. This spell is representational, and pays due deference to them for protection from harm.

You will need
- A representation of your household gods (a statue, a picture or something significant for you)
- Representations of your ancestors (perhaps a gift from a grandparent, an

heirloom, a photograph)
• Fresh flowers or taper candles
• Incense sticks of your choice
• Bowl of uncooked rice
• Bowl of water

Method

This technique offers food to the gods and the ancestors.

Place your representational objects either close to your kitchen door or near the stove, which is considered the heart of the home.

Light your incense and place the bowls in position in front.

Light the candles or place the flowers so you have created a shrine.

Spend a little time communing with the penates and the lares.

Welcome them into your home, and give thanks for their help and protection. (In Thailand, a sometimes intricate "spirit house" is provided away from the shadow of the house for the ancestors.)

Their presence is acknowledged each day so they do not become restless.

Replace the water and rice weekly.

Remembering to honor the household gods and ancestors means that their spirits will look favorably on us. Often, if there is a problem, taking it to the household gods for consideration is enough to have the resolution become apparent.

INVOKING THE HOUSEHOLD GODS

This ritual is best performed during the Waxing Moon. It could be considered a kind of birthday party, so feel free to include food and drinks as part of it.

You will need
• Pine cones, ivy, holly, or something similar
• Symbol appropriate to your guardian (e.g. a crescent moon for the Moon Goddess)
• Small statues of deer or other forest animals
• Incense that reminds you of herbs, forests and green growing things
• Green candle in a holder
• Your wand

Method

Decorate the area around your guardian symbol with the greenery and small statues.

Clean the guardian symbol so there's no dust or dirt on it. If the symbol is small enough, put it on the altar; otherwise leave it nearby. Light the incense and the candle. Stand before your altar and say:

Guardian spirits,
I invite you to join me at this altar.
You are my friends and I wish to
thank you.

Take the incense and circle the guardian symbol three times, moving clockwise, and say:

Thank you for the help you give to
keep this home clean and pleasant.

Move the candle clockwise around the symbol three times and say:

Thank you for the light you send
to purify this space and dispel the
darkness.

With the wand in the hand you consider most powerful, encircle the symbol again three times clockwise and say:

I now ask for your help and
protection for me,
my family and all who live herein.
I ask that you remove troublemakers
of all sorts,
incarnate and discarnate.
I thank you for your love and
understanding.

Stand with your arms raised. Call upon your own deity and say:

[Name of deity] I now invoke the
guardian of this household whom I
have invited into my home.
I honor it in this symbol of its being.
I ask a blessing and I add my thanks
for its protection and friendship.

You can change "its" to "his" or "her" if you know the gender of the guardian. If you have more than one guardian, change "its" to "their." Spend a few moments caressing the symbol, sending out the thought that the guardian is important to you.

Be aware of the subtle changes in atmosphere that occur as the protective spirits become part of your environment.

TO PREVENT INTRUSION INTO A BUILDING

In this spell, you use visualization and power to create a barrier to protect your home or place of business. This means that only those you want to enter do so; anyone else will be driven away. The spell can be reinforced at any time.

You will need

• The power of your own mind

Method

Sit in your sacred space and gather your energy until you feel extremely powerful.

In the main doorway of the building, face outward and visualize a huge wheel in front of you.

Put your hands out in front of you as though you are grasping the wheel at 12 o'clock and 6 o'clock, with your left hand on top. Visualize the energy building up in your hands and forming a "light rod" or laser beam between them.

Move your hands 180 degrees so they change position (right hand now on top).

Pause with your hands at 9 o'clock and 3 o'clock, and again build up a light rod between them.

As you do so, say something like:

Let none with evil intent enter here.

Again feel the energy build up between your hands and say:

*May those who would harm us
stay away.*

Bring your hands together, level with your left hip, and "throw" the energy from your hands to create a barrier in front of the door.

This powerful spell should be sufficient to prevent all intrusion, but you could reinforce it by treating all other entrances the same way. You could also visualize small wheels at the windows. You might vary the technique by tracing a banishing pentagram on the door.

PROTECTION BOTTLE

The idea behind the protection bottle is that it is made uncomfortable for negativity and evil to stay around. As you progress and become more aware, you become very conscious of negativity, while at the same time needing protection from it. This will help you achieve a good balance.

You will need

• Rosemary
• Needles
• Pins
• Red wine
• Glass jar with a metal lid
• Red or black candle

Method

Gather the rosemary, needles, pins and red wine. Fill the jar with the first three, saying:

Pins, needles, rosemary, wine;
In this witch's bottle of mine.
Guard against harm and enmity;
This is my will, so mote it be!

You can visualize the protection growing around you by sensing a spiral that has you as its central point.

When the jar is as full as you can get it, pour in the red wine.

Then close the jar and drip wax from the candle to seal it.

Bury it at the farthest corner of your property, or put it in an inconspicuous place in your house. Walk away from the bottle.

The bottle destroys negativity and evil; the pins and needles impale evil, the wine drowns it, and the rosemary sends it away from your property. It works unobtrusively, like a little powerhouse, and no one needs to know it's there.

PROTECTING YOURSELF PRIOR TO A JOURNEY

You are also in need of protection when embarking on a journey, and this simple technique will help you feel that you have an aura of protection around you.

You will need
- 4 tea lights
- Few drops of protective oil, such as sandalwood or vetiver

Method
Take a leisurely bath, placing the tea lights at the four corners of the bathtub. Add the essential oil to the bathwater.

Visualize all your cares being washed away and at some point begin concentrating on the journey to come.

Do this without anxiety; just savor the journey.

To this end, you might light a yellow candle for communication and ask to be open to enjoying new experiences, getting to know new people, and understanding the world in which you live.

You can blow out the tea lights when you have finished your bath, and relight them when you return home, as a thank-you for a safe journey.

Now prepare a charm bag with:
- 1 part basil
- 1 part fennel
- 1 part rosemary
- 1 part mustard seed
- 1 pinch of sea salt
- 1 clear quartz crystal
- Coin or bean for luck

- Square of indigo cloth
- 1 white cord

You may, if you wish, add a representation of a wheel and/or a piece of paper with the name of your destination.

Spread the cloth so you can mix the herbs quickly.

Hold your hands over the herbs and ask for a blessing from Njord, the Norse god of travel, or Epona, the Horse goddess who accompanied the soul on its last journey.

Gather up the herbs and the representative objects in the cloth, and tie it into a bag, making sure it is bound securely with the white cord.

Keep this bag on you throughout your journey.

You should find that your journey is accomplished without too much trouble, and that people are eager to assist you when you need help. You might find that you are observing more than usual, or are being asked to participate in experiences that might otherwise pass you by.

BREAKING THE HOLD SOMEONE HAS OVER YOU

This spell owes a lot to visualization and the use of color, and is in many ways a learning experience in trusting your abilities. It can be used in emotional situations, where you feel someone is taking advantage of you, or when you are bound to someone, perhaps by a false sense of duty. This technique can be done in more than one sitting, particularly if you do not want change to be too dramatic.

You will need
- Strong visual image of the link between you and the other person
- Cleansing incense (such as frankincense, copal or rosemary)

Method
Your image must be one that you can relate to. Perhaps the easiest is a rope joining the two of you together.

If you are good at seeing color, the best to use is something similar to mother of pearl, because it contains a rainbow of colors.

You might see the image as a rigid bar, which would suggest that there is an inflexibility in the relationship, which may require you to deal with the expectations of others.

The incense is used to create an environment free from other influences; this is just between you and your perception

of the link you have with the other person.

Light your incense and sit quietly, carefully considering the link between you.

Become aware of the flow of energy between you, and gently withdraw your own energy, seeing it returning to you and being used for your own purposes rather than the other person's. (This may be enough to bring about a change in your relationship, with a satisfactory outcome for you.)

Next, think carefully about how the other person depletes your time and energy—whether that energy is physical, emotional or spiritual. Resolve that you will not allow this to happen, or will be more careful and sparing in your responses. You might develop a symbol for yourself that you can use when you feel you are being "sucked in."

Use one that amuses you, since laughter is a potent tool. You could use the image of a knot being tied, a cork, or a stopcock.

If you decide you no longer wish to be associated with the person, use a technique that signifies breaking the link. How you do this will depend on your personality and that of the other person.

Visualizing the link simply being cut may bring about a more powerful ending with tears and recriminations, whereas a

gentle breaking of the link may be slower but less painful.

It is here that you must trust your judgment, with the thought that it must be done for the Greater Good. If you feel that at least some links must be left in place, you can do this; for instance, if you wish to know when the other person is in trouble.

Finally, see yourself walking away from the person, with no bonds between you.

Ensure that you leave them with a blessing for their continuing health, wealth and happiness. Now you will only become involved with them if you want to.

You can see from the above that at all points you have a choice for your course of action. This is because each stage must be considered carefully, and not done in anger. You must remain as dispassionate as you can, and stay true to your principles.

REINFORCING A
PERSONAL SPACE

In using the Goddess image as a focus, this spell is representational. It uses a mirror to represent light and power, and numerology in the nine white candles. Nine signifies pure spirituality, and therefore the highest energy available.

You will need

- Protection incense
- 9 white candles
- Round hand mirror
- Representation of the Goddess

Method

Light the incense. Place the candles in a ring around the Goddess image.

Light the candles, beginning with the candle directly before the Goddess image, and each time repeat these or similar words:

Light of Luna,
Protect me now.

When all are lit, hold the mirror so it reflects the light of the candles.

Slowly turn, ensuring you throw the light as far as you can in each direction.

Then spin around as many times as you have candles, continuing to project the light, and say:

Goddess of love, goddess of light,
Protect this space.

Pinch out the candles and put them away until you need them again.

This technique is slightly unusual in that you pinch out the candles rather than allowing them to burn down. This is because it is the intensity of light that is required, not the length of time it burns. This is a good way of rededicating your sacred space whenever you feel it is necessary.

PRIVACY SPELL

The word "occult" means hidden. While many witches have chosen to be public about their practices over the years, there is still value in the hidden, the mysterious, the occult.

Some traditions of witchcraft emphasize that it is a secret, hidden practice that is not for public consumption. They believe that your energy and power ebbs if, for example, you share a photo of your altar online. It is a belief that the sacred is special, and not for forums such as social media.

If you're feeling isolated, or you work as a solitary witch, it can be hard to feel a sense of community, and online groups often help provide a feeling of belonging. As a lone practitioner, you sometimes have to embrace the solitary, no matter how uncomfortable it feels. The ego wants you to let everyone know how powerful you are, and you may even be excited about

the wonderful results you are manifesting.

However, it's important to remember that our folklore and mythology have taboos against revealing secrets, turning back to look, or telling a real name. We even say that you shouldn't tell anyone your wish when blowing out your birthday candles, because it doesn't come true if you do.

Beyond the mystical reasons for secrecy, there is still a need in life for privacy. This spell will help with this, and should be done on a waning Moon.

You will need
- White candle
- 8 white flowers (not roses)
- Bowl

Method
Take the petals from the flowers and place them in a bowl in front of you on your altar. Light the candle, and take a deep breath in and then out through your nose. Pick up the bowl and pass it counterclockwise three times (as if making a circle vertically in the air in front of the candle). Blow three times into the bowl, imagining that all the talk and connections that no longer serve you are being blown into the bowl.

Give thanks to your patron deity, and sit in meditation a while. Snuff out the candle and discard the petals in your yard or anywhere else where they will break down naturally.

This spell releases unnecessary talk from your life and keeps your private life hidden, but you should also be aware of how you connect with others. Are you just waiting for your turn to talk, or are you really listening to what they are saying? Listening is a good way to respect others, and it will stop you from blurting out something you later regret.

CONCLUSION

Finding the magical self is a journey of exploration. As always, it is only possible to give guidelines as to what has worked for others and what may work for you. If a spell doesn't work, try it again on another occasion, and use your intuition to decide what might be adjusted to suit your personality.

The actions taken during spell-making become so personal that only you know what you did to make a technique work. For this reason, spell-making is a hidden art, and one that needs to be shared. You have the ability to make things happen, or to help in their manifestation. However, you can never be sure what the result will be. You must trust that it will be for the Greater Good. Someone else may do the same thing and end up with a different result, but one that is right for them.

If you are beginning your journey into magic, keep a journal of your thoughts, feelings, spells and rituals, as well as their outcomes. When you have found your book or Grimoire, do a ritual to consecrate it. Here is one for you; feel free to adjust it to your own tastes and beliefs. This is best done on a new or waxing Moon.

You will need
- Notebook dedicated to magic work
- White candle

Method
Bathe and dress in a way that feels appropriate to you. Light the candle and sit in contemplation of the flame. Hold the book in your lap for a while, and mentally ask Divinity or the Universe that it help you on your spiritual journey.

Open your book to the first page, and write down the first word or sentence that comes to mind. Don't think too hard about it. It might be a weird word, or what at first seems like a negative sentence or word. Don't censor or edit yourself.

Over the coming weeks, keep an eye out for anything that might help you make sense of the message of your first word or sentence. Make a note of anything that comes up. This is the start of your connection with your Book of Shadows.

As you search for knowledge, keep in mind that there are, from our perspective, certain constraints on the use of spells. They should never be used to bring harm to someone—it will only rebound on you.

You must take full responsibility for the effect your thoughts can have on others, so think carefully and be aware that, as you progress and become more proficient, spells are Words of Power.

This book is no more than a reference; we share these spells with you in a spirit of openness and freedom. If we offend anyone, we apologize. If we help someone, we are grateful. And if others find tranquility, "may the Lady and her Lord be praised."

INDEX OF SPELLS